A Daily Gift of Kindness

A COLLECTION OF STORIES FROM KIND
HEARTS AROUND THE GLOBE

Teresa Velardi

Published in the United States of America

Interior Design by Ambicionz

Spirit Book Endeavors
c/o Authentic Endeavors Publishing
Clarks Summit, PA 18411

A Daily Gift of Kindness
ISBN: 978-1-963849-59-2 (Paperback)
       978-1-963849-60-8 (eBook)

A Prayer for Kindness, Compassion, and Forgiveness

Father, kindness, compassion, and forgiveness describe Your character. How can I be more like You, Father? How can I be an outlet of Your kindness, compassion, and forgiveness to the people You have purposefully placed in my life? Show me, Father. Open my heart to remember the words of my Savior and feel the all-encompassing love of You, my heavenly Father. I am loved, chosen, purposed, and forgiven. Therefore, encourage me to pray, live, and love in a reflection of these great truths about who I am. Guide my prayers and my life. Let all I do, honor You. In Jesus Name, Amen.

Choosing kindness, happiness, and joy can transform your perspective and the impact you have on others. It's a beautiful way to approach each day: decide to be happy, decide to be kind, and decide to spread joy. Be the pebble that creates positive ripples in the world, imagining how small actions can lead to significant change. It's a powerful reminder that every kind act, no matter how small, can spread and inspire others. Think about the specific ways you can "be the pebble" in your community, turning your decision to be kind into actionable steps - whether through volunteering, random acts of kindness, or simply spreading positivity in daily interactions. Every effort counts. Share your ideas and plans at TeresaVelardi.com

Dedication

*Sometimes, it takes only one act of kindness and caring
to change a person's life.*
Jackie Chan

To all those who need to experience a gift of kindness
and
To all those who are kind enough to give one.

Kindness is a conversation that makes a difference.
Teresa Velardi

Table of Contents

Acknowledgments

There are many moving parts and many helping hands that work together to put a compilation book together. Each one is essential to the process.

Thank you to every contributing author who shared a story in this book. Each one is a blessing to me and each of the readers. Together, you have set the table for the reader to enjoy a vast buffet with which to fill their heart and soul. We can all taste and see the warmth and goodness that comes through every aspect and story of kindness.

Doreen DeJesus-Harper, thank you for your commitment to this project. The countless hours you have spent setting up systems and ensuring that all the pieces are put together in what seems to be an endless box of puzzle pieces has brought forth a beautiful book. You are a blessing!

Aljon Inertia, no project would be complete without your touch. Thank you for all you do.

Mary Vovers Brown, thank you for your creative spirit. Your joy is alive and well on some of these pages.

Alison Treat, thank you for your expertise in editing. You are a gift.

To each person who reads these stories, thank you for taking the time to read and hopefully share this collection with others who will also benefit from the kindness of others.

Scatter seeds of kindness everywhere you go!

A LITTLE Kindness CAN CHANGE THE WORLD

Foreword

by P.J.

We live in a time dominated by haste, conflict, and a relentless pursuit of self-interest—a time when kindness might be considered a lost art. And it's in this exact moment of our social evolution when genuine, heartfelt kindness is most needed to keep people feeling connected—and our world more peaceful.

Simple expressions of patience, compassion, and generosity are not just moral niceties—they're essential threads in the fabric of our shared humanity. For those of us who believe deeply in kindness, kindness is not a luxury to be shared when all is right in our world, but our most natural—and sincere—way of being when interacting with anyone of any age in virtually any setting.

One of the most elegant aspects of kindness is the beautiful coupling of patience and forgiveness. At its highest level, this marriage affords grace to the difficult people in your life—those who seem overwhelmed or consumed by their fears and struggles—and, unfortunately, take them out on others.

The genuinely kind person understands their struggle and acts with patience, specifically intending to alleviate their suffering—and further offers forgiveness, allowing the person struggling a certain grace if they wish to apologize or begin again.

Please understand this does not mean kind people allow themselves to be walked on, disrespected, or taken for granted.

Kindness does not constitute weakness. In fact, sincere kindness in the face of offensive and hurtful intentions, pettiness, and blatant disrespect demonstrates unbelievable self-control over an instinctual need to fight back and protect yourself.

Whether the kindness you show others is your default reaction to another's unkind behavior—or a conscious and intentional effort—may not matter. What matters in those seemingly difficult moments with others is that you are demonstrating, leading, and engaging with your integrity and commitment to kindness!

Exchanging one unkind word or gesture for another is an emotional echo. Echoes repeat and reverberate far from their initial point of origin, meaning if you get trapped in an ongoing exchange of negativity, it doesn't just impact you and your antagonist. It ripples outward and influences other innocent people you're connected with.

And it's the same with kindness—it's just that the ripples left from kindness make the world a more positive and pleasant place for everyone to live.

Kindness is one of the most powerful forces in the world because of the profound impact it can have on people's lives. It's been known to save lives, feed the hungry, connect with people who feel unlovable, and that's just getting started!

As someone who is physically disabled, I've experienced firsthand how kindness can change lives. I have thrived, not just because of my own resilience, but because of the kindness of others—family, friends, and even complete strangers. Their willingness to help, to show compassion, and to offer support has made all the difference for me.

Within my life, I have had 3 or 4 people tell me they were planning on taking their own lives until they spent some time with me and began to feel as if someone—me, in those moments—genuinely did care about them and that helped them to feel like they mattered. In those conversations, they reconnected with a sense of value, and life became worth living again. That is the power of kindness!

I was completely unaware of their intentions until they shared that my kindness saved their lives. Knowing my genuine caring and sincere kindness saved someone's life humbles me beyond measure. It brings me to my knees and fills my heart and eyes with tears of gratitude!

Your experiences with kindness—whether giving or receiving—are equally important because every story where kindness plays the starring role is beautiful!

When we begin to look at the myriad of opportunities each of us has for kindness and the delicious ways we can be kind to one another, we realize they're truly uncountable. This liberates the kind person to be as authentic and heartfelt as possible because there seem to be infinite ways to personalize your expression of kindness and connection with others.

Kindness is an elegant kaleidoscope of creativity and can be expressed in more than just a way that impacts someone's emotional state. It has the power to transform someone's financial life, strengthen their faith, heal relationships, and even improve their physical health. How you choose to share it is quite often a very personalized gift, which is one of the reasons kindness touches us so deeply.

When someone receives virtually any act of kindness, it tends to feel as if it was specifically intended for them; it feels as if it's carrying a message, "I see you, and you matter."

Too many people in today's world get lost in the shuffle and become exhausted in obligations, leaving them feeling invisible and unimportant—and, to a genuinely kind person, this can be heartbreaking. So, the empathy that kind people share with the sad, lost, and lonely strengthens the fabric of our co-existence and lifts the spirit of those who may have otherwise been lost.

For someone feeling forgotten, unloved, uncared for, or unworthy—in any way, for any length of time—to feel seen, heard, understood, and cared about can, honestly, be an absolute lifesaver for some!

It's like the sun, all of a sudden, breaking through the clouds on a cold, gray day. When that sunlight settles on your skin, it instantly warms you up and relaxes your body, mind, and spirit. To the recipients of your generosity, it may feel like they can take a breath for the first time in what feels like a long time. Your kindness transforms their energy—much like Spring transforms our world with new possibilities!

Throughout this introduction and book, you will read about how we can become increasingly kind to others, and how kindness can make the world a better place by nurturing strangers and loved ones. It's filled with heartfelt stories of how kindness impacted the authors' lives and how it formed and strengthened relationships.

While these stories and insights will be delicious to your heart and soul, I would like to leave you with a simple reminder: be kind to yourself, also!

You've heard this said before and likely even offered some version of that advice—but do you live with it? Do you practice kindness, patience, and forgiveness with yourself when you make a mistake, fail to follow through, or are just feeling out-of-sorts for some reason?

And if you do, do you practice kindness regularly—and in all areas of your life: physical, mental, emotional, spiritual, financial, and social?

While the introduction may not be designed, nor intended, to address the kindness-to-self question with any real depth, it would be remiss of me not to share a simple how-to as my contribution to your relationship with kindness.

When you focus on yourself, it's important to suspend any judgment or expectation and just allow yourself to feel what you feel.

I encourage you to put your attention in your heart area—physically resting the palm of your open hand on your chest often supports and stimulates the tender emotions associated with kindness. Feel free to close your eyes if it helps you connect with your emotions and the soft, physical sensations ignited by your feelings.

As you focus on feeling a kindness or gentleness in your heart area towards yourself, notice you feel a general sense of peace, patience, and forgiveness. Notice how your mind quiets down—and how your breath has become relaxed and more naturally full. Allow yourself to relish in these delicious and deserving sensations.

When in this state, you may feel rich emotions that lead you to cry— a little or a lot, especially if you don't regularly receive this kind of nurturing from others. Embrace these feelings; these are tears of gratitude. Stay with them, and don't run them off; just feel your feelings.

This book is intended to inspire you to see the world—not just as it is, but as it could be—a place where empathy, compassion, and love are not the exceptions of the day but the norm. We sincerely hope that you will be moved by the collaboration and effort these beautifully kind authors and souls have put into this book—and that you will continue to share kindness with every breath.

Kindness gives birth to gratitude; gratitude establishes healthy connections, and healthy connections lead to more kindness.

We hope you enjoy this book and it touches you deeply!

P.J.

Introduction
Three Simple Things

Teresa Velardi

I n a world that seems more divided and confused than ever, how can we survive and thrive through whatever comes our way? In this incredibly divisive time we are living through, three simple things can change how you look at what's happening around you, within you, to the people beside you, and ultimately, because we are all connected, what's happening in the world. What are they?

I'm glad you asked! Gratitude, Hope, and Kindness. The first two books of the Daily Gift Book Series have many stories written by many contributors.

This book brings us to the third "simple thing" that can change everything...Kindness!

What exactly is kindness?

Webster says it's "the quality of being kind." Okay, but what does it mean to be kind? Again, Webster says: a) of a sympathetic or helpful nature, b) of a forbearing nature: Gentle.

The Bible has many verses about kindness. Here are a couple of my favorites:

"But the fruit of the Spirit is love, joy, peace, longsuffering,
kindness, goodness, faithfulness, gentleness, self-control.
Against such, there is no law."
Galatians 5:22-23

"But love your enemies, do good, and lend, hoping for nothing in return; and your reward will be great, and you will be sons of the Most High. For He is kind to the unthankful and evil."
Luke 6:35

Kindness can change someone's day or even their entire life. I've seen many circumstances turned around by one person simply being kind to another. If you are kind to others, they will be kind to you. Well, most of them will. There will always be those who 'just don't get it.'

In this book, you'll read many stories about ways to be kind, stories of being blessed by the kindness of another, and a few reminders to be kind to yourself. There are also examples of "Pay it Forward."

Paying it forward is a great way to be kind to many. There have been multiple incidents of people driving through drive-thru venues and paying for the order of the person behind them. The driver is surprised to learn that their order has already been paid for, so they pay for the next person, creating a "chain" of kindness and giving.

If you think most people wouldn't do that, you'll be surprised to learn that the longest line of this kind was more than 900. Yes, nine hundred people paid for someone they may not have known.

These three simple things are life-changing. I promise you this. Life will be better if you wholeheartedly practice gratitude, live hopefully, and are genuinely kind to yourself and others.

The Kindness of Strangers

by Alysia Lyons

Imagine waking up from a deep slumber, unsure if the smoke you're smelling is real or just part of a dream, only to realize it's your worst nightmare. Your phone rings—it's your neighbor, frantically yelling, "Dude, your house is on fire!"

You leap out of bed and wake your wife and kids to rush them outside. Then you rescue the dogs.

What else should you grab? The tools you use to make a living? The collectibles you've listed to sell for some extra cash?

"You can't go in there, man!" a uniformed stranger warns. "It's not safe."

Seconds later, the roof collapses—right where you would have been if that stranger hadn't stopped you.

Tears stream down your face as you stare at the rubble that was once your home. The place where you were raising your children, the house you scrimped and saved for seven years to pay off early.

"I don't have fire insurance," you think.

Neighbors and strangers drive by, staring at the empty space where your house used to stand.

"Here, man." One passerby hands you a check for $500. "Take this, I'll be back with more."

"I own a construction company," another man says. "I'll level this land for you for free."

Women from the community gather clothes for your family. Within hours, they have a whole new wardrobe to replace what was lost.

"I never believed in God before," you think to yourself. "But today, I experienced His love through strangers."

Kindness – A Profound Impact

by Sally Mary S. de Leon

T he world unfolds before me like a sprawling city with untold stories. Amidst towering skyscrapers and hidden alleyways, I'm drawn to the quiet corners where kindness takes root, where a single act of compassion blooms like a wildflower through concrete.

It's not the grand monuments or flashing neon signs that captivate me but the subtle, unspoken gestures and acts of grace illuminating the human spirit. Like a hidden garden amidst the urban sprawl, kindness offers sanctuary—a place to breathe and reconnect with our shared humanity.

I remember discovering a community garden between towering apartment buildings. Amidst the rows of vegetables and fragrant herbs, people from all walks of life worked side by side, sharing knowledge, laughter, and their harvests. It was a reminder that kindness can flourish even in the most unexpected places.

Scientists tell us kindness impacts our well-being, releasing endorphins that calm our minds, reduce stress, and foster inner peace. It strengthens our social bonds, reminding us we are part of something larger than ourselves.

I've seen its transformative power in countless encounters—in a stranger's tender touch, a friend's comforting words, and the selfless acts of a passerby. Kindness is a language understood by all, a universal balm soothing the world's wounds.

I invite you also to choose kindness. Choose to nurture the gentle flame in your heart, to let it guide your path and interactions. In a world that often seems harsh and unforgiving, kindness is the refuge we seek, the love that binds us together.

BE BOLD
BE BRAVE
BE HUMBLE
Be Kind

The Trash Day Dash

by Mary Vovers Brown

J ust before dawn, as I swim out of slumber, I hear the familiar low rumble of the garbage truck. Bleary-eyed, I spring out of bed. It's a holiday. Usually, they don't pick up on holidays.

Yesterday's get-together filled our bin with prawn shells from the feast. It's not a pleasant addition to our hot garage. I open the front door and see the garbage truck passing by. I race to the garage, grab the bin, and, with my nightgown billowing in the wind, take off after the truck.

Just then, my new neighbor appears, dragging her bin. She's in full pajama glory—white fuzzy bunny slippers and all. Together, with our bins, we race down the street. We don't quite catch the garbage truck, but we stand there in our sleepwear, laughing at the absurdity.

Turns out, her name is Denise. As we get acquainted, I say, "I can't believe we missed them!"

Denise laughs, "Looks like we've got great timing!"

"At least we got to meet in style," I reply with a grin.

Just then, the garbage guys—bless their hearts—come back. They saw us in their rearview mirror. We cheer like we've won the lottery, laughing and clapping in relief. I feel an unexpected wave of emotion. The kindness of these garbage collectors not only saved my family from a week with an odiferous garage, but they also helped me connect with my new neighbor. Who knew trash day could be so heartwarming? Or so hilarious?

A Hand to Hold

by Alyssa Ruge, Esq.

After 20 years as an attorney, something rarely shocks or surprises me. I've encountered and handled situations that most would find overwhelming, earning a reputation for being unshakable. However, a few years ago, I was introduced to an entirely new side of the legal system, one I had never experienced: the dependency court and foster care system. Nothing could have prepared me for what I saw.

A few years back, my daughter's teenage friend was removed from her home due to false allegations. Instead of being placed with relatives or friends, she was sent to a group home. Despite offering to foster her myself, I was disqualified because I had known one of the alleged perpetrators - someone who was falsely accused.

I found it ironic, as an attorney with a spotless record, that I wasn't qualified to care for a child due to a casual acquaintance. Yet, I was allowed to visit her in the group home and take her on outings. We went to the mall, visited a tearoom, and I helped her replace stolen personal items – all taken during her short time at the group home.

This experience fueled my determination to become a licensed foster parent in Florida. So many children, from infants to near adults, desperately need safe, loving homes as their family situations are being resolved. Whether it's temporary care or a permanent placement, offering shelter can make an immeasurable difference in a child's life. If you can provide a home, please consider becoming a licensed foster parent. It's one of the most impactful and rewarding acts of kindness you can do.

BE·KNOWN
For Your
KINDNESS
And Grace

The Warmth of Winter's Guardians:
A Tale of Unsung Heroes

by Amanda Beth Johnston

I n the depths of winter, when biting winds cut through layers of clothing and snowflakes obscured vision, a group of unsung heroes stood unwavering. These guardians of our children's safety braved the elements day after day, their dedication a beacon of hope in the chaotic morning drop-off.

Amidst the swirling snow and rumbling engines, they orchestrated a symphony of protection. Each child was known by name, their stories etched in the hearts of these individuals. Some children needed extra hugs, and these compassionate souls provided them without hesitation, their warmth starkly contrasting with the frigid air.

With nothing but a metal sign, they faced down the massive trucks, their courage a shield for our little ones. As I watched my children's eyes light up at the sight of them, gratitude overwhelmed me. These extraordinary people weren't just doing a job, they were nurturing the future.

As the holidays approached, I felt compelled to express my appreciation. I gathered simple gifts, hoping to convey my heartfelt thanks. On the last day before winter break, I distributed my tokens. The surprise and joy on their faces melted the winter's chill, warming my heart.

At that moment, I realized the profound impact of small gestures. These winter guardians had shown us the true meaning of kindness, and in return, we kindled the flame of gratitude in their hearts. Their unwavering commitment had not gone unnoticed, and in recognizing their service, we all grew a little warmer, a little kinder, despite the winter's cold.

"Too often, we underestimate the power of a touch, a smile, a kind word, a listening ear, an honest compliment, or the smallest act of caring, all of which have the potential to turn a life around."
Leo Buscaglia

Special Delivery Kindness

by Andi Buerger, JD

T he doorbell rang. Instead of a neighbor, I was greeted by a lovely woman holding a stunning bouquet. She wished me a wonderful day and departed. Tucked inside the beautiful arrangement was a tiny card. Although it seemed generic at first, the message it carried is forever engraved in my heart.

The surprise delivery was from a young woman I had never met, but had spoken with just two months after my beloved fur baby, Dusti, had entered that special place where all good dogs go at the end of their earth days - puppy heaven!

Dusti was more than just a 'good' dog. She was extraordinary in every way, offering unconditional love and even therapy to my family and the hundreds of at-risk homeless teens we rescued. A Golden Retriever with enviable corn silk colored hair, Dusti won the hearts of even our toughest teens. She was my first and only pet, my constant companion, and my husband's second favorite "girl." Everyone fell in love with her engaging spirit and spunk. Whenever Ed and I traveled, Dusti would stay at a local pet resort. She was and still is the only dog they ever allowed to stay behind the desk to greet incoming guests.

After 15½ years of love and devotion, it was I who made the decision to let her leave this life with dignity. The loss was enormous. When Chewy.com called regarding an autoship of toys and treats I had forgotten to cancel, I shared Dusti's story with the young woman on the phone. Her tender words on a tiny card remind me how special that delivery was, even to this day.

"A kind heart is a fountain of gladness, making everything in its vicinity freshen into smiles"
Washington Irving

What Kind Are You?

by Anne O'Brien

T he other day, I was walking our dog, Eddie. He's been particularly curious about a little rabbit he befriended in our backyard. On this day, we observed him snacking on clover.

"Hi, Mr. Bunny," I whispered. "What kind of rabbit are you?"

He looked up at us with a half-eaten piece of clover hanging out of his mouth. "I'm the kind that brings a smile to your face. What kind are you?"

Eddie did his biz, and we went along.

Later that day, I hurried off to the grocery store, intending to get two items and ending up with twenty. I scurried to the checkout. A man whose face was etched with years of weathered wisdom stood to the side, holding two fruit platters.

"Sir, would you like to go ahead of me?"

He thanked me, explaining that he was going to be late getting to his granddaughter's house. He'd thought of using the self-checkout, but it went against his ethics.

"People need jobs," he said, "and I have a hard time supporting an automated replacement."

We exchanged a few more pleasantries. He paid and scurried off.

As I paid for my groceries, the memory of my dad flashed in my mind's eye. Dad was kind and considerate and loved nature. I stuffed my credit card in my wallet and the gentleman's token of thoughtfulness next to it as a reminder to pay it forward.

I could not wait to get home and talk to Mr. Bunny.

"You can accomplish by kindness what you cannot by force."
Publilius Syrus

Volunteering Makes a Difference

by Teresa Velardi

C hristmas was just around the corner. A friend and I went to
Ronald McDonald House to bake cookies for the families
there. A couple of kids were excited to help us. We sang carols and
talked about what was on their Christmas list. Their brother had suffered
life-threatening injuries in an accident and was staying in a nearby
hospital. We did our best to engage the kids in decorating cookies. We
had a good time together, making the most of a very stressful situation.

When I got home, I realized I'd left my bracelet behind. I called the
house to let them know I would pick it up the next day. When I arrived,
the mother of the boy who had been in the accident greeted me. "I'm so
grateful you were here yesterday," she said. "My son had a wonderful
time with you. You girls took his mind off his brother. It was the highlight
of his Christmas. His brother passed away last night, and the joyous time
he spent with you made a real difference. I can't thank you enough for
your kindness."

With tears in my eyes, I hugged her and expressed my condolences
for her loss. She handed me my bracelet. It was engraved with, "With
God, all things are possible." God had allowed me to share joy amid
great sadness.

Volunteering is an act of kindness. Always be kind. You never know
what's going on behind someone's smile.

Kindness Won

by Dr. Anne Worth

Arriving at Walmart around 10 pm, I noticed a large, disheveled man near the entrance. I asked him if he was hungry. "No, Mama, but water sure would be real nice."

I brought him a cold bottle of water and returned to tackle my shopping list. When I came out with a cart of groceries, he immediately arose and asked, "Can I help you, Mama?" I hesitated.

But a still, small voice told me to accept his offer. I learned his name was John and walked to my car side by side.

I popped open the trunk, and John piled my groceries into it. "Mama, you will never know how your trust lifted me tonight. I been feeling pretty low these days, thinking I was of no use to nobody. But you let me walk with you and help you. You made me feel right good about myself."

Tears sprung into my eyes when I realized I could have rejected his offer. I wondered how many people walked past him that day. I could have been one of those people if I had let our differences make my decision.

As I drove away, I remembered the scripture about giving a cup of water. And I reminded myself, when God tugs at your heart . . . Listen.

John and I felt pretty darn good that night. Kindness won.

How Wide is Your Smile?

by Debra Costanzo

T he world is hurting. It seems people are hurting more now than ever before. Every day, we meet people who feel emotionally bankrupt. The clerk at the register may have just lost a parent. Our waiter or waitress may have just lost a child. And we wonder why they are not bubbly.

We are all vying to be noticed. To be heard. To be validated. To feel loved and accepted. We think we must make grandiose gestures for someone to feel these deeply desired affections. We think we must write a profound self-help book, or give an inspiring talk, or donate to a highly visible charity claiming to meet the needs of various people. These are all noble acts of kindness.

But...

We forget how far a smile reaches. We hurriedly pass people every day, never smiling, never saying hello. When I smile and say hello, most people look scared. They look at me suspiciously. Often, I feel I should apologize right after I say "Hello." That's how far we've come from true community. But I do it anyway.

Ah...there's a word! Community. We talk about building "community."

We throw that word around like an over-chewed dog's bone. We overcomplicate it. Our friendly smile and warm greeting can often turn a person from feeling hopeless to hopeful; from invisible to noticed; from rejected to accepted.

Look behind you. Look ahead. Smile and say hello. Someone needs only one friendly smile and one warm greeting. You will make their day!

IN A WORLD WHERE YOU CAN BE ANYTHING •

♥BE KIND♥

From Poverty to Prosperity

by Donna Franklin

G rowing up in extreme poverty, life was all about survival. There was no room for dreams, only the gnawing question of where our next meal would come from. The only consistent food was at school—weekends were a void of hunger. My siblings, my grandmother, and I often starved. But I refused to let poverty define my future.

Right after high school, I left the place I was born, determined to build a life beyond the shadows of my childhood. What I have achieved since then is beyond anything I could have imagined. For two years, I felt a nudge from God, and when I finally listened, I knew my mission: to ensure no child would face weekends of hunger like I did.

That's when I started a program to send food home with kids for the weekends, ensuring they and their siblings wouldn't starve. Five years later, we've fed over 2,000 children locally, and I want to make this a nationwide program.

I also wrote *Developing Your Kick-A** Mindset,* a national and international bestseller, to inspire others to overcome their challenges. Proceeds from the book help fund this initiative, ensuring it continues to grow and touch more lives.

Everything I endured as a child shaped my purpose today—to feed, to uplift, and to ensure no child feels the hunger I once knew.

"I've learned that people will forget what you said, people will forget what you did, but people will never forget how you made them feel."
Maya Angelou

The Woman Who Made Me Feel Seen

by Fran Asaro

K indness has surrounded me throughout my life—both the kindness I've given and the kindness I've received. Like many of us, I experienced one act of kindness that impacted and reshaped me.

When I was ten years old, I attended my aunt's wedding. I grew up in a loving home, but like most children at the time, I was treated as a child, spoken to in a way that matched my age. However, on that special day, something shifted.

I was seated at a table full of familiar faces, but to my left was a woman I had never met. Lorraine was a friend of my aunt's. I never saw her again, but Lorraine changed my life.

Amid the music, laughter, and joy, she took time to connect with me in a way I had never experienced. She treated me like a friend, not just a child. We talked, we laughed, and I felt seen and heard in a way that made me feel important.

I don't remember our conversations—maybe about school or the wedding —but I do remember how she made me feel. Lorraine's kindness left an imprint on my heart, and here I am, nearly sixty years later, still grateful for her.

Who has given you that moment of kindness? Who did you generously give it to? Who still remembers you, thanks you, and is a different person because of you?

Remember those people. Be one of those people.

Have you had a kindness shown?
Pass it on;
'Twas not given for thee alone,
Pass it on;
Let it travel down the years,
Let it wipe another's tears,
'Til in Heaven the deed appears
Pass it on.
Henry Burton (1840-1930)

Courage to be Kind

by Ida Ra Nalbandian

A loud explosion filled the neighborhood. A dark cloud of smoke appeared with fiery flames. Mesmerized, I watched the lid of a manhole fly into the air and fall with a thunderous bang. I gasped audibly.

Our street is commonly busy with cars passing by. By a celestial miracle, there were no cars on either side of the street then, and I wondered, "Where are all the cars and pedestrians?"

Our neighbor, Zvia, rushed fearlessly out of her house and stood before the fiery flames. As cars appeared, she signaled them to detour, avoiding the danger.

Frozen in awe, I thought, "Wow, what a courageous lady! She put her life in danger to save others!"

Being ill for several months, Zvia could not walk. *Where did that strength come from?* What phenomenon is this?

On their arrival, firefighters discovered faulty wiring had caused the explosion. Once the police blocked the street, Zvia barely walked home, leaning on the fence. *Where did her strength go?*

Zvia's courageous kindness and lack of injuries were the miracles I had just witnessed. I wondered what cosmic force held back those cars that usually would be roaring down our street. Clearly, the invisible power of kindness itself protected us.

I'm grateful to have witnessed the glorious courage and kindness of my neighbor, Zvia.

Kindness is a power that does not seek any rewards or recognition while expressing itself as it is: a backing aid from the divine when our circumstances arise and necessitate it.

Love is patient and kind; love does not envy or boast;
it is not arrogant or rude. It does not insist on its own way;
it is not irritable or resentful; it does not rejoice at wrongdoing,
but rejoices with the truth. Love bears all things, believes
all things, hopes all things, endures all things.
1 Corinthians 13:4-7

The Kindness of Family and Spirit Sisters

by Ilene Gottlieb ~ The Heart Healer

I've lived alone for many years and appreciate the peace and quiet, especially in the early morning hours. Sitting in the kitchen with my coffee, I love listening to the birds' songs and watching palm fronds move with the breeze, squirrels jumping from branch to branch, beautiful blue skies, and neighbors walking with puppies in tow.

Creating a peaceful life is a gift of kindness only we can give ourselves. But what do we do when we experience significant trauma or illness, and we're unable to take care of ourselves?

Last year, I was so ill that lying in bed was the best I could do for the better part of three weeks. The idea of having to navigate my way through this illness alone was traumatic. Fortunately, I didn't have to do it on my own.

Without being asked, my family and dear spiritual sisters "went to work." They delivered specially cooked foods, orchids to bring cheer, almost daily text messages to check in and to share their love, and so much more. Their kindness was palpable, and I will be forever grateful for all of them. I know without a doubt that their loving kindness helped me to heal.

The gift of kindness keeps on giving, especially when it's shared. I pray that you, too, have people in your life to bless you with kindness and that you can do the same for them.

Surrounding you with love ~ Ilene

Ho'Oponopono ~ I love you, I'm sorry, Please forgive me, Thank you.

Be Kind Be Brave Be Bold

My Father's Gift of Kindness

by Jacki Long

My father taught me the simplicity of kindness. He demonstrated ease and comfort in showing others love through gifts, kind words, and genuine service, without expecting anything in return. He gave freely to my mother, his in-laws, students, to me. Especially notable was Dad's unwavering support of his abusive parents.

Dad treated people equally. He didn't discriminate, offering equal treatment toward women, the poor, service workers, clerks, and strangers. He offered drinks to all who entered our home, and I continue this practice today. To my disbelief, an elderly contractor teared up when I said he could take any drink he wanted from my refrigerator, revealing that no one had ever offered him a drink while working in their homes. This was incomprehensible to me.

Dad was present whenever I asked, making himself available to watch our kids, run errands, and lend his wise ear. He was present even when I didn't ask, paying for my kids' schoolbook rentals, taking my car in for service, and humbly offering advice while respecting my choices. He showed up every day of my life, present at every sporting and musical performance, tirelessly chauffeuring me to piano lessons and school events, and tutoring me in the expertise of writing and grammar.

Dad's wit and sense of humor were cornerstones of his existence. One left his presence with a smile or a giggle, feeling elevated. He thought of others before himself until the day he entered his final, ill-fated heart surgery, attempting to unburden others as his body failed him. His final days were spent on a ventilator, machines keeping him alive. Each day was a labor of losing hope that he could return to the life he desired. We gave our selfless, compassionate husband, father, grandfather, and friend the ultimate gift in return for a life serving others. We let him go.

The Glimmer

by Jill Clay

There I stood, lost in my reflection—eyes clouded with unshed tears, carrying the weight of the untold pain of rejection. The mirror before me wasn't just glass; it was a portal to my soul. My eyes, once full of life, now reflected the weariness of a heart burdened by despair. I felt trapped in my sorrow, unable to see past the darkness.

In that sacred moment, I stared into my own eyes. I did the only thing I could—I prayed. "Lord Jesus, please." It wasn't a grand prayer but a desperate whisper, a plea for light in my pain. And in the silence, something extraordinary happened. The Holy Spirit met me there, in my brokenness. A faint glimmer appeared in my eyes. I could see and feel it—a spark of hope, a sign that God hadn't left me even in my despair.

That glimmer grew as I allowed His presence to wash over me. Once a reflection of my pain, the mirror became a reflection of His love and grace. I began to see myself not through the lens of fear but through the eyes of the One who loved me beyond measure.

God transformed my sorrow into strength. That fragile smile on my lips was the sign of my soul healing and my spirit being renewed.

What do you see when you look in the mirror? God sees beyond our pain and wants to show us the light of His grace.

Carried by Kindness

by Joyce Waring

W hen I picked up the phone that dark January evening of 2020, a kind but serious voice said, "You have cancer." The optimistic doctor continued," You will need surgery, but hopefully that will be all."

Stunned, I found my husband, Steve, outside and told him the news. With his arm around me, we walked back to the house to talk about this journey we were about to embark on. Weeks passed, and after several hospitalizations, I was home and starting to recover, minus my right kidney. Then came the phone call saying it was an aggressive form of cancer, and I would benefit from twelve weeks of chemotherapy.

Two sweet friends, Katie and Carrie, put together a big surprise package to get me through this ordeal. Secretly, they talked to each member of my family and many friends from church, then gathered items from each person. I received a large album filled with encouraging cards and well wishes, a glittery box with twelve goody-filled drawers (one to be opened each week prior to my treatment), a countdown chain with Bible verses from my grandchildren, a cheery photo album from my daughter to be enjoyed during my six-to-eight-hour treatments, and much more. Such kindness! To top things off, Steve was my chauffeur and stood by me through it all. I was blessed by their loving kindness and thank God for His care and faithfulness during this storm in my life.

Give thanks in all circumstances...
1 Thessalonians 5:18a (RSV)

The Box with the Golden Ribbon

by Kate Rohauer

I came home from school and saw a present on the dining room table. It was wrapped in white tissue paper, sparkling gold ribbon, and a giant bow. In our world, gifts were few and far between. We were very poor, and we didn't celebrate birthdays or holidays. My mom asked me to leave the gift at her friend's house, knocking on the door and running away.

I wished Mom would give me a gift like that! The following Sunday at church, crying tears of joy, the friend asked people who left the present.

I whispered, "Aren't you going to tell her?"

Shaking her head no, she pointed to Matthew 6:3, "When you give to the needy, don't let your left hand know what your right hand is doing." Then Acts 20:35, "It's better to give than to receive."

Mom had been studying the Bible with this friend and invited her to church. She said she had nothing to wear. Mom had been saving change to buy a black velvet dress for a special dinner she was going to that winter. Instead, she bought the muumuu her friend was now wearing. That's what was in the box!

Just over a year later, Mom died from ALS. She was thirty-five. I realized then that she had given me a present after all. Wrapped by her love and kindness, she taught me that the Golden Word of God was a priceless gift that would keep on giving the rest of my life!

*"Remember there's no such thing as a small act of kindness.
Every act creates a ripple with no logical end."*
Scott Adams

Mrs. Amalia

by Katerina Pappas

L ove has many hues—kindness is one of them. The defining characteristic of kindness is that it is often initiated by those from whom we least expect it.

When I was around six years old, my class went on a field trip to a botanical garden.

I grew up in a bilingual household and attended Greek school, so I didn't always know the correct words to use. Thus, I preferred to stay quiet.

I remember how excited I was to be outdoors in an environment where we could learn about flowers, trees, and plants. But that excitement didn't last long.

At the end of the field trip, all the kids stopped by the gift shop to buy plants to take home. I felt sick to my stomach because I knew that I did not have enough money to buy anything.

My first-grade teacher, Mrs. Amalia, discreetly came up to me. In a very delicate manner, she told me I could pick out any flower I liked and not worry about the price.

I felt as though a guardian angel had come to my rescue.

I chose a simple plant with a red bloom. She paid for it without anyone noticing, and then we all got back on the bus to return to school.

Her act of kindness stands out nearly thirty-five years later. I am forever grateful to her for gifting me such a sweet memory and for having empathy for a little girl's heart.

"When you are kind to others, it not only changes you, it changes the world."
Rabbi Harold Kushner

Vessels of Kindness

by Linette Rainville

Whoever is generous to the poor lends to the Lord,
and He will repay him for his deed.
Proverbs 19:17

I've learned that it's impossible to out-give God. Whenever I can, I love leaving an outrageously generous tip for a waitress or buying coffee for the person behind me in line. But kindness doesn't always involve money; it can take many forms, like offering a smile, complimenting a stranger, or investing time in others.

You may have heard the saying, "God gave us one mouth and two ears so we can listen twice as much as we speak." Lately, I've been making an extra effort to be generous with my listening, slowing down to truly hear and see the people I encounter.

It might be a cashier at Walmart, a janitor emptying trash cans, or my doctor, busy with a stack of paperwork. Their reactions are often one of surprise when I ask, "...and how's your day going?" Demeanors soften, faces brighten, and a genuine connection is made. It's truly miraculous how a small act of kindness can make someone feel valued, appreciated, and seen.

Becoming a vessel of kindness means waking up each day determined to make a difference in someone else's life. If we take the time to look, we'll find opportunities everywhere to be generous with the gifts God has given us - and when we do, we must prepare our hearts to be blessed in return.

"The best way to find yourself is to lose yourself in the service of others."
Mahatma Gandhi

Is Kindness a Choice?

by Mark O'Brien

D riving to a dental appointment one summer day, I was stopped at a traffic light. A woman began crossing the street in front of me. She had a cane and looked as if she might be mentally challenged. When she got to the middle of the road, she fell, hitting her head on the pavement.

I put my emergency flashers on and jumped out to help her. She was conscious but not responding. As I cradled her in my arms, some firemen from a nearby station rushed to her aid. Knowing she'd be in better hands than mine, I thanked the firemen and walked toward my car. Then I noticed my forearms and hands were covered with blood.

I drove to the dentist's office. The receptionist gasped when she saw the blood.

She called for the dentist, who came out to the front desk with a hygienist. They accompanied me to their wash-up room and started scrubbing my hands and arms with Betadine sponges. As they scrubbed, I told them what had happened.

The dentist asked, "Why did you do that?"

"Because if I'd been the one lying in the road, someone would have stopped to help me."

Is kindness a choice?

Sociopaths and narcissists notwithstanding, I believe all of us are wired to care for each other. It's not an intellectual decision. It's a reflex. If someone is harmed or in danger, we act.

I don't know if that's kindness, but I have absolute faith in it.

Kitty

by Dr. Kate Keville

One summer, I faced a heartbreaking loss: my two elderly dogs and my cat, all beloved companions, passed away. My heart shattered, and I promised myself I wouldn't bring any more animals into my life.

Then, one cold night, a tiny, emaciated kitten stumbled up to my door, crying softly as I sat on my back porch. I fed her, reassuring her that I'd find her a loving home, but I made it clear she couldn't stay with me. I searched for a permanent home for her, yet she remained by my side as the months passed.

I received a scholarship for a month-long writer's retreat two years later. I arranged for a friend to care for Kitty during my time away, but within two days, my friend called to say she'd run away. His home was over fifteen miles from mine, and the news broke my heart. When I returned a month later, there was no sign of Kitty. I missed her terribly and called out for her every night, hoping against hope.

Eight months later, on a quiet evening, as I sat on my porch, I heard a loud meow in the darkness. I peered out into my yard—and there she was. "Kitty, is that you?" I called. She bolted into my arms, her body thin and scruffy, tears streaming from her eyes. Somehow, she'd found her way back.

Kitty stayed with me for twenty-one more years. I'll never forget how she made her way home, nor the resilience and love she taught me along the way.

A little more Kindness a little less JUDGEMENT

A Daughter's Farewell: Memories of Kindness

by Brenda Warren

T he salt-tinged breeze whispered through Myrtle Beach, the sun painting the sky in hues of gold and lavender. I clutched the urn containing my father's ashes. This beach had been our sanctuary, a place where the world melted away, replaced by shared laughter and quiet moments of reflection. We escaped here as often as his battle with cancer allowed, each trip a cherished memory.

Our tradition began with a stop at the quaint fabric store. Next was the cozy diner, our go-to spot for comfort food and heartwarming conversations. Each location offered memories of my father's kindness.

Finally, I stood at the water's edge, the ocean mirroring the vastness of my grief. As I prepared to release my father's ashes, a couple approached, their eyes filled with empathy. They offered words of solace, a comforting hand on my shoulder, and shared their own stories of loss and healing.

With a final goodbye, I scattered his ashes, a gentle cloud of love carried by the wind. I turned to thank the couple, but they were nowhere to be found. A sense of wonder filled me—perhaps they were angels. As I made my way back, I reflected on the couple's random act of kindness now forever etched in my heart.

I discovered a renewed sense of purpose that day. The world felt a little less lonely, a little brighter. The couple's kindness had planted seeds of resilience within me, a reminder that life, in its fragility, held beauty and grace.

Your Life Matters

by Chantay Bridges

Y ou never know what a day will bring. That morning, I arrived to see a car surrounded by piles of belongings, as if someone's whole life had been tossed out. No one was around at first, but soon, a woman appeared. She was older, limping, and clearly overwhelmed by the sheer amount of things she needed to move. There weren't enough dollies available, and the one I had was in use. I approached her and offered help, though she politely declined at first. Still, I could see she was struggling.

Determined to assist, I offered her my dolly and unloaded my things so she could use it. It turned out she had been kicked out in the middle of the night with no warning and nowhere to go. Her belongings were thrown onto the sidewalk, and despite her pleas, she was treated cruelly.

Moved by her situation, I reached into my purse and handed her all the cash I had. Overwhelmed, she began to cry, thanking Jesus and calling me her angel. When she counted the money, she realized it was exactly what she needed to secure a new place. Her gratitude was overwhelming and brought tears to my eyes as well.

As I was leaving, she told me I was her angel. I smiled and said, "God bless you." It's a reminder that we can all be someone's angel, extending kindness. One small act can make a world of difference. Turn a stranger into a friend; our mission, the Lord's extended hands.

BE·THE
Reason
SOMEONE
Smiles Today

Kind with an "I"

by Chevi Price

Seekin' through fair eyes
Using senses of wariness
Feelin' tension of unkindness.

No one knows the unknown
Judgin' by the appearance
Not knowing each story entwined in the moment.

Stories upon stories
Captured through daily experience
Exceeding through emotions.

*Less patience
Deeply breathing
Anger upon others.*

Where one second moment
Switches an off button to some
That causes those heated moments.

What we seek of ourselves
We seek in sight
Where it teaches true colors of not only others but ourselves.

It starts with seekin' in
Diggin' deep in the darkness
Within the strongest emotions.

Negativity is fused in the brains
Fewer and fewer smiles upon faces
Entwined with less understanding what life is for each human.

Society takes away the light
Where no one shows comfort
But hate that spreads like butter.

A smile
A hello
Asking about each other's day.

What we send to others
Will teach the "I" in kindness
Where we can teach ourselves.

Saying "I"
Taking the power
That changes how we seek the inside.

Where we seek positivity
We seek guidance
That attracts a better society.

Where more light be brought
Seekin' smiles through the darkness
Where kindness wins all in the end.

Guided by Grace: The Kindness That Inspired My Success

by Dr. Givonna Cheeks

"A single act of kindness throws out roots in all directions,
and the roots spring up and make new trees."
Amelia Earhart

From childhood, I envisioned building and leading my own thriving business. After retiring from the United States Military, I set out to bring this dream to life in the competitive world of government contracting.

I proudly launched my company and landed my first subcontract with a state government agency in 2018. The following year, I secured a federal subcontract. I soon realized how much I still had to learn about this field's complex rules and protocols.

During this phase, I had the great fortune of meeting Mrs. Gale LeGrand Williams, a successful, seasoned business owner. We instantly connected over shared values, faith, and a mutual love of fashion. With her warmth and wisdom, Gale became my mentor and "big sister." Despite her demanding schedule, she generously carved out time to guide me through the intricacies of government contracting—from mastering proposal responses to sharing invaluable lessons she'd learned along the way.

Gale's kindness has left a lasting impact on me. In the high-stakes world of government contracting, it's rare to find someone who offers unwavering support. I truly believe each of us has a unique path destined by God. When we lead with kindness and integrity, there is no need to fear competition. Gale's selflessness has inspired me to pay it forward to other business owners as my company grows.

"No act of kindness, no matter how small, is ever wasted."
Aesop

Inspire Kindness

by Gloria Sloan

W hat does kindness mean to you?
We know it involves being friendly, making people happy, and doing the right things. It is a behavioral action that makes us care, be helpful, and be considerate. Kindness comes in different forms that don't look the same for everyone. Yet, we know what it feels like when we receive it. Empathy, acceptance, thoughtfulness, and gestures allow us to experience the gift of generous, inspired kindness.

Kindness is acting without expectation of reciprocity or recognition but with genuine compassion for humanity. It is an understanding of where a person is on their life journey. When I was an active Rotarian with Rotary International, we were encouraged as members to practice kindness and acts of service. We organized initiatives to provide humanitarian service and advance goodwill by volunteering to help the needs of the community and society. Through those acts of inspired kindness, I better understood circumstances impacting someone else's life journey.

Kindness is not just a fleeting act but a movement with a lasting impact. People can, and most will remember, acts of kindness for a lifetime. Be inspired to pay it forward to keep the kindness moving. Kindness is love. It is selfless and unconditionally inspiring when practiced. The more you do for others, the more you do for yourself. The benefits of kindness last long after the act for those who offer kindness. It can improve self-esteem, strengthen relationships, and be a key part of growth and personal development. Inspired kindness can increase feelings of well-being and happiness.

"The smallest act of kindness is worth more than the grandest intention."
Oscar Wilde

The Power of Words

by Anonymous

P aul was the kind of person who kept to himself. He would nod politely but rarely engaged with others. Everything changed the night Steve, his best buddy since High School, opened up to him. Steve had returned from combat, a shadow of the vibrant person he once was. Steve sat across from Paul with tears in his eyes and a tremble in his voice.

"I was going to do it, Paul," Steve whispered. "I was walking toward the bridge, ready to end it all. I felt invisible like I didn't matter to anyone."

Paul sat very still, his heart pounding in his chest.

Steve continued, "I made a deal with myself. I wouldn't go through with it if just one person acknowledged me. People kept passing me without a glance. But then, a stranger looked right at me and said, 'Hello' with a small smile. That moment, that tiny bit of recognition, saved my life."

Steve's words hit Paul like a tidal wave. He realized how fragile life could be and how powerful a simple gesture could become. From that day forward, Paul made it a point to greet every stranger he passed on the street. It didn't matter who they were or where they came from—each person received a warm, sincere "Hello" from him. Paul knew the value of being seen and acknowledged. And maybe his small acts of kindness would ripple out into the world, spreading happiness and offering hope to someone else on the brink.

"Carry out a random act of kindness, with no expectation of reward, safe in the knowledge that one day someone might do the same for you."
Lady Diana Spencer, Princess of Wales

Majestic Spectacle

by Christopher Crouse

T he morning began as always, with the sun rising slowly behind the trees like an advancing army. Tree shadows stretched like a militia of mighty giants, only to retreat as the sun climbed higher. This majestic spectacle plays out each day, but my circumstances and thoughts remain the same. How will I feed them? Christmas is approaching, and I have nothing for them.

I reminded myself not to worry and that God had everything under control. I questioned my decision to move my family for a part-time youth pastor job and restart my contracting business in a new place. Did I do the right thing? Was I following God's path for me? Thoughts flooded my mind. Yes, of course I did, I thought.

I didn't share my worries with anyone, not even my wife. I'd wake up every morning, get ready, and pray while watching the sunrise from my truck. Then, I'd drive around, introducing myself and passing out business cards, hoping for work.

Christmas Eve arrived, and I wondered what kind of dinner we'd have. I only had a few small gifts for the children. They're young; maybe they'd be happy with the toys.

At 7:30, after the children fell asleep, there was a light knock at the door. Three women and an older man stood there with an entire Christmas meal and a truck full of toys. Who were they, and how did they know?

That year, the greatest Christmas gift I received was kindness.

KIND
PEOPLE
Are my
KIND OF
PEOPLE

The Joy of Kindness

by Johnny Tan

What does *"Kindness"* really mean? Is there such a thing as *"Degrees of Kindness?"*
Wouldn't that be something interesting to ponder? Over the years, acts of kindness have brought me tremendous joy. My mom taught me that our conscious action in responding to a situation of wanting to be helpful and assist others is sparked by our divine nature within us. Whenever the opportunity arises, our subconscious operates unselfishly to nourish and contribute to our spiritual superpower.

My latest experience of kindness occurred last week and was a definite joyful moment. It was that time of the evening when I had to rush to the local 7-Eleven to buy my Powerball ticket. Upon arriving, I saw a couple in their late sixties working on their car battery as the hood was up. They were still at it when I came out after buying my ticket. They were trying to remove the old battery without success. I walked over and offered them the use of my jumper cable to start the car so the lady could drive to the nearest auto store to buy a new battery. The gentleman, her brother, had driven five miles to help her.

After hooking up my jumper cable to her car battery and his truck, we successfully got her car running again. Although I didn't win the Powerball that night, the genuine thanks and loving handshakes I received were the *"Kindness Jackpot Win"* for me. I had contributed to their happiness and smiled my way to sleep.

KINDNESS is Essential

Kindness at Christmas

by Karen Booze

When our children were young, we went through a season of severe financial hardship. We were barely getting by, and as the cold weather set in, we realized our oil tank was nearly empty, with no way to fill it. The deacons at our church stepped in, offering to cover the high cost of heating oil and filling our tank. Accepting such a generous gift was difficult, but we were in desperate need.

A few weeks later, the head deacon showed up at our door with bags of Thanksgiving food for our family. I explained that we would spend Thanksgiving with relatives and didn't need a meal. But he insisted we keep the food to feed our family for a week or two - another humbling experience that left us feeling seen and loved.

As Christmas approached, my husband began crafting small wooden gifts for our children in the garage. Just before the holiday, we were approached once more by the same man, who told us that someone in the church wanted to bless our children. On Christmas morning, there were homemade gifts my husband had made with love and store-bought presents gifted anonymously.

Though still young, our children were old enough to understand our financial struggles. They also grasped the significance of someone outside the family providing these gifts. For years, they shared how meaningful this experience had been for them. This extraordinary act of kindness revealed God's love for our family profoundly and unforgettably.

Throw
KINDNESS
around Like
CONFETTI

Teaching Kindness

by Katie Lesesne

I lost my job and decided to try to substitute teaching to earn money while searching for my next permanent job. There was a school within walking distance of my house, so I chose to take an assignment there to teach a Special Needs classroom. Most classes that I had subbed for had a lesson plan already established. The regular teacher had left permanently, so I needed guidance telling me what to do with this class.

I fumbled around for the first half of the class, looking for things I could give the students. Three assistants were in the class, and at first, no one said anything. I thought this would be my last time in the classroom since I had never taught before and had no idea what I was doing.

When Ms. Clayton spoke up, things finally began to work out for me. She gave me worksheets to hand out to the class and told me which students could do them. Ms. Clayton became my guide, showing me how to run the class and learn what lessons students could handle. She even put together lesson plans for each individual so I would know what to assign the students throughout my time there. Ms. Clayton is the only reason I had a successful teaching experience.

Have Courage AND be kind

A Beacon of Light in the
Sea of Darkness

by Kristin Aurelia

I n my darkest hour, the kindness and compassion of a stranger served as a beacon of light in my greatest time of need!

I sat in the doctor's office and realized that no answers made medical sense. I had seen many specialists as mystery symptoms and conditions permeated my body, with no answers in sight. I was alone, surrounded by nothing but a sea of darkness. My health was deteriorating rapidly. I was staring death in the face, and the spiral of fear and hopelessness grew stronger each day.

During this time of uncertainty, I was introduced to an extraordinary woman. In our initial conversation, I could feel her kindness and compassion as she patiently listened while I shared my story. She offered an alternative approach that required a lifestyle change and commitment. I was determined to live, so I agreed to listen. This was my introduction to the Medical Medium protocols.

New to this space, I struggled with understanding the various protocols. We spoke often, and I always felt seen, heard, and supported. When I was well enough to travel, I had the opportunity to meet her in person and express my gratitude. That visit was magical. The wisdom, knowledge, and friendship we shared created a bond I will cherish forever.

The gift of kindness from a stranger has inspired me to pay it forward along my journey.

"Kindness is the only service that will stand the storm of life and not wash out. It will wear well and be remembered long after the prism of politeness."
Abraham Lincoln

Unlocking Potential: A Journey of Growth and Kindness

by Linda Weller

Fresh out of high school, I landed my first "real" job in a mailroom. I quickly became known for my efficiency and knack for finding ways to improve processes. I worked late, took work home on holidays, and never asked for overtime. I just wanted to get the job done. The owner noticed my dedication and asked if I knew anything about computers and if I was interested in learning. I jumped at the chance, eager to see how this new knowledge would allow me to improve our systems further.

I took college courses with the company's support and attended numerous IBM training sessions. Eventually, the owner entrusted me with designing the new computer room for our new building. Armed with graph paper, I meticulously planned the layout, placing computers and printers to scale. When the room was completed, it matched my design perfectly. This project led me to become a Database Administrator and later a programmer—all thanks to an owner who saw potential in a young person and took a chance.

Years later, I shared this story on a panel at a major conference in Atlanta. I was overwhelmed by how many people reached out to me afterward, sharing how much it resonated with them. It made me realize the power of kindness and believing in others' potential. That experience shaped who I am today; the confidence it instilled has stayed with me ever since.

"Nothing can make our lives, or the lives of other people, more beautiful than perpetual kindness."
Leo Tolstoy

Kindness Always Wins

by Lori Walker

*"We are each of us angels with only one wing, and we can
only fly by embracing one another."*
Luciano de Crescenzo

I t could have been any ordinary Thursday. I walked into the
Huddle House in Hinesville, Georgia, and ordered a turkey bacon
club. I held back hot tears as I reflected on the conversation with my mother
earlier that morning.

It was Thanksgiving Day, 1988. I had left my conservative childhood
home a month after my eighteenth birthday to marry my high-school-
sweetheart -turned-US-Army-soldier. After a year of marriage, I walked
away. He had been unfaithful while I worked nights at a fast-food restaurant.

Frightened and alone, I desperately searched for meaning in the chaos
surrounding me. Little did I know, my own "Army" of Angels was waiting
for me in my coworkers at Wendy's. I was astounded to discover the levels
of diversity, support, and acceptance extended to me from wise,
experienced military families.

My first two Angels were Tina and Felicia. Like Mother Hens, they took
me under their wings and guided me with gentle grace. Later, I met three
more Angels—Tammy, Tim, and Marisol. Today, the four of us are still
friends.

Exactly one year after my Huddle House meal, I was invited to
Thanksgiving dinner at Joann and Jesse's home. By then, I had found love
again. My new man was cordially invited as well.

I'll never forget those early years. My Angels revealed that love is
unconditional.

Kindness always wins.

"Kindness is the light that dissolves all walls between souls, families, and nations."
Paramahansa Yogananda

A Friendship from Across the World

by Mariena Johnson

S ocial media platforms like Facebook and Instagram have opened up new ways to share information and connect with people around the globe. A straightforward friend request nearly a decade ago became a lifelong friendship and sisterhood. It began when my mom accepted a friend request on Facebook from a young woman in the Philippines who had met one of my friends during a mission trip. She reached out, and my mom became her second mother before long.

Out of curiosity, I accepted her friend request as well. Could I genuinely get to know someone living halfway across the world? We began communicating. She shared details of her life - living without running water, using dirt holes as restrooms - yet, despite her circumstances, she remained so positive and kind. We exchanged messages, pictures, and videos, updating each other regularly. Since we're all Catholic, my mom taught her essential lessons like paying tithes.

Over the years, our friendship blossomed into something incredibly inspiring and refreshing. My Filipino friend decided to become a registered nurse, and my mom offered to help by paying for her tuition. Now, she's just one year away from earning her BSN in nursing. She is such a fantastic woman and has inspired me in countless ways. I can't wait for the day she finally comes to the USA so we can meet face-to-face.

Madel Angel Garo - I'm so grateful to know you and have grown with you over the years. You are an incredible inspiration, and I love you dearly, Sis.

Kindness Poem

by KB

Kindling an action, so sweet and selfless
It's energy burning bright, creating a shockwave of
Never ending ripples
Donations for the desperate, compliments for the lost
Never ending ripples, from one soul to another
Every life changes; ashes to ashes, day-to-day
Singing a grateful harmony across the stars
Similar in tune and cadence

always
Be
Kind

Kindness Grows Kindness

by Michelle Harwood-Lange

K indness is a gentle sister of compassion. In a world that is fast becoming cruel and harsh, we need more of this virtue. Some years ago, the Universe and God gave me a phrase: "Kindness grows Kindness."

In 2005, on the heels of losing a child, grief shrouded my life with an ooze of fog that suffocated any kindness. In a hospital, engulfed by depression, my husband stood over me in devoted prayer, beckoning me with God's power to return from the brink of death.

His act of kindness awakened me. I needed to find loving kindness for myself to become whole again. That journey began with accepting my loss with tender grace, choosing to leave behind the unhealthy behaviors, and creating building blocks of kind self-care every day. I pivoted the loss into an anchor to discover joy, love, celebration, and most of all, kindness for myself again. We cannot give from what we do not have within us.

Over the years, I have felt waves of joy as I participated in acts of kindness. Being generous, considerate, compassionate, accepting, and friendly toward others doesn't take much. It is a simple way we can build hope in our communities. The Beatles said it well: "All we need is love." I say that all we need is kindness, too.

As we are kind to ourselves, our actions, thoughts, and choices are kind to the earth, each other, and life.

75

Kindness

by Pastor Jack Rehill

I n the Holy Bible, Galatians 5:22 says that kindness is one of the fruits of love produced by the Holy Spirit. It is not human kindness that comes from our humanness. Why do I say that?

Human kindness only goes so far. It is limited to those who deserve it—an eye for an eye; a tooth for a tooth. However, spiritual kindness goes much further because it comes from love—agape, the highest form of love. The Greek word agapé (ἀγάπη) is defined as "undefeatable benevolence and unconquerable goodwill that always seeks the highest good of the other person, no matter what they do or what they're like."[1] It is the self-giving love that gives freely without asking anything in return and does not consider the worth of the person.

The Greek word for kindness born out of the love of God is chréstotés (χρηστότης), which means "goodness in action."[2] It speaks of acts or words of kindness toward another. Sweetness of disposition. Gentleness in dealing with others. The word describes the ability to act for the welfare of those taxing your patience. Those who get on your nerves. Those you would rather avoid. It is unconditional just as the love of God is unconditional. It treats those taxing your patience just the same as those who don't tax your patience.

1 Corinthians 13:4 says that love is kind. May we know and show the kindness of the love of God more and more.

---

[1] Jack W. Hayford et al., *New Spirit-Filled Life Bible: New International Version* (Nashville: Thomas Nelson, 2015).
[2] Jack W. Hayford et al., *New Spirit-Filled Life Bible: New International Version* (Nashville: Thomas Nelson, 2015).

The Ripple Effect of Kindness

by Rutez Mason

Being kind is a simple gesture that can go a long way, touching the recipient's heart. I remember a time in my life when kindness made all the difference. After my second son was born, he was diagnosed with over 100 allergies and zinc deficiency, which caused a severe skin condition. He required constant care and attention, as he was prone to skin infections.

When he was six months old, I was accepted into nursing school. I knew this was God's plan for me, as it was challenging to get into these programs then. But I didn't have the resources, and I had no idea who would take care of my sick baby. That's when a lady from my church, who knew about my son's condition and my acceptance into school, stepped in. She said, "I'll keep your son while you go to school."

Peace came over me because she was well-known for caring for children. Thanks to her kindness, I was able to finish nursing school. God blessed me with a career, and I eventually became a Director of Health & Wellness. Years later, I could offer the same kind of support to others. Several young ladies who worked for me, raising children independently, would call to say they couldn't come to work because they had no one to watch their kids. So, I took care of their children while they worked. I could ease their minds, just as that kind woman from my church had done for me.

"No kind action ever stops with itself.
One kind action leads to another.
Good example is followed. A single act of kindness throws out roots
in all directions, and the roots spring up and make new trees."
Amelia Earhart

Racing Against Time
to Say Goodbye

by Rev. Maj. Sandra Kitt

A warm sensation flowed through my body as the plane landed in Houston, TX, and I knew it was the moment my brother Kim died of AIDS. He spent his final days in Hospice as I awaited a call from them telling me when to come say goodbye. The call came too late for me to make it in time.

Kim decided to stay in Austin, TX., after I had been transferred to Germany with the Army. Luckily, at the age of 30, he was adopted as an "emotional love project" by six to eight people in an outreach group from a local church. The members talked, sang, and played games with him. As his health deteriorated, they made sure he had everything he needed.

While on leave from the Army, I had five days to make cremation arrangements, clean out his apartment, and say my final goodbyes. I met each team member at dinner the first night and heard about their favorite Kim memories. They assisted and supported me every step of the way during this difficult time. Members picked me up at the airport, gave me a place to stay, and several helped me clean out his apartment.

During a memorial service they arranged at their church, I loved hearing their favorite stories of Kim. I am so grateful to know that loving people surrounded him, and he did not die alone. The generosity of these complete strangers humbled me.

I will be forever grateful for their kindness.

Resource: A Wink and A Prayer: A Vet's Near-Death Experience

"Start everything with kindness and the end will be okay."
Elijah James Knight

Rediscovery

by Shaheda Daya

When you hit rock bottom, the only way is up. Right? I hit rock bottom. All the signs were there, and yet I did not prevent it. It was meant to happen. I was dealing with anxiety and depression.

And so, the journey of rediscovery began with the first step—therapy. But that was just the beginning...

I chose to go down this path because I had never traveled it before, and I truly believed many answers would be provided. I had many questions about past events from which I never healed. I had questions about my values and why they were important. I wanted to know my purpose in life.

I may never reach the destination, yet I learned much on this journey. In order to learn, we must trust ourselves on any path we take. Being honest with ourselves is fundamental. Fear can be our unknown ally as it brings growth. We are never in control of our circumstances, but we can learn to surf the waves of life and ask ourselves, "What have I learned?" This is gold.

So, what is the goal? If we say self-actualization, what does this mean for you? Where is the sweet spot when we feel alive, grateful, and happy?

These are some of the questions I can leave you with to invoke some real reflection. I certainly hope they send you in the right direction!

"A kind gesture can reach a wound that only compassion can heal."
Steve Maraboli

Be Kind. It's Really Not That Hard

by Angi Currier

I Bought a shirt with this saying on it, and I thought how powerful those words are. We are living in a world of such hatred and negativity, but I believe that when you spread kindness, it will come back to you. Paying for someone's meal at a restaurant or purchasing a coffee for the person behind you at the coffee shop sets a friendly tone. It puts a smile on someone's face—it might be their only smile that day. It also sparks the thought of paying it forward. Helping an elderly lady push her grocery cart to her car only takes a few minutes out of your day. Kindness can be as simple as a smile.

When you see someone grieving the loss of a loved one, hug them. If an addict is struggling to stay clean and sober, give them words of encouragement. If you see a homeless person trying to keep warm, give them a blanket. If someone wants to do something for you, let them. They are being kind.

I love the holidays, especially Christmas. It seems people tend to spread cheer and try to keep the miracle of giving alive. Life is too short not to be kind. There is no reason to be grumpy and negative all the time. Go out there, spread some love and joy, and see what it does to your soul. You will be amazed at how good you will feel.

kind IS THE NEW cool

The Kindness of a Smile

by Eileen Bild

*The magic of a gentle touch and smile is what
could transform someone in the moment.*

I have always had a positive demeanor and love to spread "pixie dust." There is something incredibly uplifting when kindness is spread sincerely, not expecting anything in return. In times of need, sometimes a gesture as simple as a touch or a smile will make all the difference in someone's life.

Did you know that it takes fewer muscles to smile than to frown? The benefits are infinite—you immediately feel better, and it can spread like wildfire. This infectiousness brings joy and happiness, overriding all other emotions. A daily practice of smiling improves attitude while reflecting outwardly on the world.

Smiling brightens my day and gives me a sense that everything is okay. When I see sadness in others, I want to soothe their sorrows. In my experience, the compassion that comes through a smile is golden.

We live in a world where joy and happiness are most beneficial for emotional and mental health. If you consciously walk out the door, radiating your inner light, it sends magic into the air. Something happens within the universe that attracts more of the same, providing memorable positive experiences.

Every day, I see opportunities to compliment others, smile, and say thank you. My relationships are stronger because an unseen connection is formed through kindness, showing I care, and letting others know they matter. This is the gift that keeps on giving.

ALWAYS SPREAD KINDNESS

My Gift from God is Bob

by January Liddell

For over 25 years, Bob has been a true blessing in my life. He is a remarkable soul, one of a kind. From the beginning, Bob has been a constant source of kindness, always willing to lend a helping hand without expecting anything in return. I vividly remember when he offered me my very first video client. At the time, I was starting and struggling to make ends meet. Bob saw my need and, without hesitation, connected me with someone who could help me earn a living. That simple act of generosity changed the course of my career, and it's just one of many examples of his thoughtfulness.

Bob's kindness goes far beyond the professional. He opened his home to me when I needed a place to stay. He made me feel welcome, loved, and supported. He created a space where I could focus on building my future. His generosity extends to everyone in his life, not just me. He sacrificed his career and social life to be his mother's caretaker. He constantly showers my children with gifts and extends his brotherhood to my husband, ensuring we always feel loved and valued.

Bob's consistent kindness, care, and selflessness inspire me every day. He has an innate ability to see where help is needed and gives of himself freely. Bob has been a gift, leaving an indelible mark on my life. He embodies what it means to care for others, and I am endlessly grateful for his unwavering friendship and support. Bob is forever family to me - my hanai (Hawaiian meaning adopted) brother - truly a gift from God.

KINDNESS
is free
SPRINKLE
that stuff
EveRYwhere

The Magic of Your Smile

by Renée Isermann

Every morning offers a fresh chance to make a positive change in your life, and it can start with something as simple as your smile. Your smile is more than just a reflection of joy - it keeps you feeling youthful, radiant, and connected to your inner peace. It carries a quiet strength that can open doors in ways you might not expect.

When you wake up tomorrow, try standing in front of the mirror and smiling at yourself. Notice how it spreads warmth through your body, lifting your mood and bringing light to your day. Ask yourself: What thoughts lift me up? What brings me joy?

Your smile cannot only transform your energy but subtly influence the world around you. When it comes from a place of inner peace and self-compassion, your smile becomes magnetic, naturally drawing love and peace into your environment.

This practice of intentional smiling is at the heart of what I call the Smile Revolution. By embracing simple Yoga4Face® techniques, you can reveal your unique beauty and, in turn, help make the world a brighter, more beautiful place.

Be kind to yourself and others—let your smile be the quiet force that transforms your life and gently touches the lives of others.

I Choose Kindness

by Sally Mary S. de Leon

T he world is a symphony of joy and sorrow, love and loss, each note resonating with the human experience. Amidst this ever-changing melody, I'm drawn to the enduring power of kindness—a steadfast flame burning even in the deepest darkness. It's not grand or fleeting but a quiet echo of the soul, a gentle touch mending the fractures within us.

Kindness is not a grand performance but a quiet echo of the soul that can transform the harshest landscapes into fertile ground for hope. I've seen it in a child offering a hand to a fallen friend, in the embrace of a loved one offering solace in grief, and strangers reaching out with open hearts. These moments remind us of the inherent goodness within us all.

But, oh, the sting of tears when kindness meets indifference, an outstretched hand is met with a closed fist, and a gentle voice is drowned out by a world that has forgotten how to listen. In those moments, the heart aches for the lost opportunities to connect, heal, and love.

Yet even in sorrow, kindness persists. It is the unwavering ember refusing to be extinguished, the quiet reminder of our shared humanity. A single act of kindness can illuminate a brighter tomorrow.

So, I choose kindness—a source of light and warmth, a steady hand reaching out to those lost and alone. It is the redeeming power of love and enduring hope in a world that can seem cold and unforgiving.

"She opens her mouth with wisdom, and the teaching of kindness is on her tongue."
Proverbs 31:26

Pay It Forward

by Teresa Velardi

W hile returning from an appointment thirty-five miles from home, I was almost out of gas, with no cash or credit cards. I could picture my purse sitting on the counter in the kitchen. I'd left it behind in a rush to get my young son to the babysitter. There wasn't enough gas to get me back to him. I was running on empty.

When I stopped at the nearest gas station, I asked if I could call someone to use a credit card over the phone. The guy immediately said, "No, we don't do that." Pleading didn't help. I returned to the car and began the fruitless search for money that may have fallen between the seats, under the mats, even in the trunk. I only found a few coins, mostly pennies. I closed the door and rested my forehead on my arm against the roof. I asked aloud, "Now, what am I going to do?"

Just then, a man approached me, reaching out with a five-dollar bill. I stood there with a puzzled look on my face. He said, "Go ahead, take it. I heard you talking to the clerk. Take the money, buy the gas, and get your son."

I asked for his address so I could pay him back. He said, "No need - pay it forward." I thanked him profusely and promised to pay it forward. And I have - several times. The kindness of a stranger created the ripple effect of paying it forward.

*"But love your enemies, and do good, and lend, expecting
nothing in return, and your reward will be great, and
you will be sons of the Most High, for he is kind
to the ungrateful and the evil."*
Luke 6:35

A Circle of Love and Kindness

by Theresa (Terry) Scarborough

When I think of acts of kindness done out of love, care, and beautiful friendships, I can't help but remember the time when my husband, Gary, was very sick with cancer.

We were moving from our two-story home, packed with 30 years of memories, to a much smaller place near our daughter. With so much to sort through and pack, we were overwhelmed. Friends, neighbors, and family members stepped in to help without us even asking. Some tasks we couldn't have done without their help.

At that point, Gary was too ill to do much, and I was struggling as well. But around twenty beautiful souls from different areas of our lives came together to help us empty the house and move to our new home. Their generosity was nothing short of amazing.

Even after Gary went to Heaven, some of these friends continued to show up, helping me with yard work and repairs at the new house. I will forever be thankful for this outpouring of love and the way they surrounded us with care during such a difficult time.

Indeed, I am thankful for the Lord's blessings.

"Kindness can become its own motive.
We are made kind by being kind."
Eric Hoffer

The "Write" Kind of People

by Tyra Glaze

*When you have complete faith in your vision, the right
people will be drawn into your life.*
Ms. Moem

After overcoming Breast Cancer, I knew I wanted to share my story with the world. At twenty-nine years old, with two young sons, being told I had Triple Negative Breast Cancer was a tough blow! However, I still wanted to have Courage and Kindness. My life began to change as I embraced being the "Fierce Warrior" I was destined to be. I wrote my first blog post, "Fierce Fight," in July 2020, and it was published on the Susan G. Komen Blog to inspire others around the world.

In 2021, I reached out to a publisher for the first time about publishing a children's book. I'm a very private person, and that is one of the reasons I hadn't sought a publisher before. I'd already written my story, but I needed help with the next steps. It turned out that this publisher, Teresa, and illustrator, Aljon, were indeed the "write kind of people!"

Teresa and Aljon are genuine. They helped me share my story through my children's book, *My Mom is My Hero*. Throughout my publishing journey, they had compassion and understanding. During our virtual meetings and phone calls, we built a relationship and showed empathy toward each other. We were kind, thoughtful, and authentic. I'm thankful for the "write kind of people," and that we had the pleasure of working together to share my story!

'Wrapped in Rainbows' of Kindness

by Will Pollock

I f kindness could be a walking, talking human, it would be Valerie Boyd. Valerie was a fabulously successful, award-winning author of the acclaimed Zora Neale Hurston biography "Wrapped in Rainbows" and mentor to dozens of erstwhile authors, journalists, and writers of color hungry to impact society for good. She was my dear friend and champion, radiating a signature luminescence in a cynical world.

"So, Will. Are you ready to be on Oprah?" she asked before I presented my book "EIQ: Emotional Intelligence in Men" at her "Art of the Book Proposal" seminar (2008). That event was a seminal moment in my life. I made lifelong friends, Valerie included. I discovered a new purpose after working for years as a corporate writer and commercial photographer.

Our bond endured long after the seminar, with frequent book-strategy sessions over coffee and meals. When one of her longtime colleagues asked Valerie for up-and-coming authors, she recommended me. I, in turn, sang her praises to anyone who would listen! I stayed in touch with authors from the seminar, many of whom have attained great success on their own. When my son Cam was born on Valerie's birthday, I texted her as a new, sleep-deprived dad to say, "We now have two December 11th souls destined for greatness."

Valerie Boyd, an accomplished essayist, Atlanta Journal-Constitution editor, and hometown Atlanta hero, lost her battle with cancer in 2022. In my contribution to this collection of kindness stories, I believe Valerie would want me to say this:

"Kindness is more than a noble characteristic: it's an act of audacious empathy meant to inspire people to reach for, and attain, their better selves."

BE KIND
And
COURAGEOUS

Radiating Kindness: The Art of Nurturing Yourself

by Amanda Beth Johnson

In our fast-paced world, the importance of embracing kindness toward ourselves is often overlooked. Yet self-kindness is essential for overall well-being and personal growth. It's about treating ourselves with the same compassion we freely offer others.

Self-kindness begins with a shift in mindset. Acknowledge our imperfections and accept them without harsh judgment. Instead of self-criticism, we can practice self-compassion, seeing our shortcomings as opportunities for growth.

A key aspect of self-kindness is prioritizing self-care. Taking time to recharge—whether through meditation, pursuing a hobby, or simply resting—nurtures our physical and mental health. It equips us with the resilience and strength needed to face life's challenges.

Equally important is setting healthy boundaries. Effectively recognizing and communicating our limits is a key aspect of self-kindness. It protects our energy, allowing us to meet our needs without feeling overwhelmed or burnt out.

To cultivate self-kindness, try keeping a "Kindness Journal." Each evening, jot down three things you appreciated about yourself that day—small achievements, acts of self-care, or moments of resilience. This simple practice encourages positive self-talk and reinforces a habit of gratitude toward yourself.

By celebrating your achievements, no matter how small, you nurture a sense of accomplishment and motivation to continue striving for your goals. Incorporating self-kindness into your daily life enhances self-esteem and improves your relationships with others. Treating yourself with kindness builds a foundation of love and respect that radiates outward, contributing to a more compassionate world.

Kindness Grows in Layers

by Fran Asaro

L ife lessons often start at an elementary level, and as we grow, these lessons deepen and expand, enriching our wisdom and understanding. Take honesty, for example. As children, our first experience with honesty is that we learn not to steal. Later, we might learn to return money that we found or received that didn't belong to us, and so on, until honesty becomes a core value woven into the fabric of who we are.

Kindness works in a similar way. We may learn kindness as a simple act when we're young, such as sharing toys or food. As we commit to it and practice it, it sinks deeper into our being. We give authentic compliments and acknowledgments. As it progresses, every level we grow in kindness is exhilarating because it moves from something you *do* to something you *are*. People may not always see your kind acts or remember exactly what you did, but they'll never forget how you made them feel.

Being kind becomes a quiet, powerful force that radiates from within. You don't have to announce it or seek recognition, yet people will feel the warmth of your presence. That's the beauty of kindness. It's less about being noticed and more about the energy you bring to the world.

Consider becoming a scholar in kindness. Experience the richness of its benefits and feel how it changes the way you perceive the world. It is truly one of the most rewarding feelings.

Smoke in the Air

by Joyce Waring

A new house, a September evening and a party on the patio above the Deschutes River. Darkness was falling, and the guys were sitting around the outdoor fireplace while the gals cleaned up from dinner in the kitchen. The children were in the living room enjoying a movie, when suddenly the house started filling with smoke.

Stifling panic, I calmly ordered the ladies to retrieve their purses and get everyone outside. Apparently, the roof had been burning for quite a while from a construction defect in the flue. After dialing 911, I ran around trying to find hose bibs in the dark, all the while crying and praying. The fire trucks came, and we ended up with a total tear down of our new house. Neighbors Dick and Jane came to the rescue and allowed us to stay overnight and gather our wits.

The next day, while viewing the damage, neighbors Bob and Lynn, whom we had never met, drove by and suggested we move into their vacation home just below us on the river. They wouldn't be using it, as they were headed back to their vineyard in San Luis Obispo. What a blessing. We lived there free of charge for more than a year while rebuilding.

Bob and Lynn would come on occasion and throw large dinner parties, and we would be invited to join in the festivities! Such kindness! They will always hold a special place in our hearts. God bless you, Bob and Lynn.

"Be Kind to one another, tenderhearted, forgiving one another, as God in Christ forgave you.
Ephesians 4:32

The Kindness of Strangers

by Mary Vovers Brown

From above, I watch her struggle, her heart heavy with grief, each step weighed down by the sorrow of loss. Her days blur together as she makes the arrangements. She moves like a shadow of herself, trying to numb the unbearable truth. She lives in a haunted nether world, imagining a last breath, a last thought, a release of spirit now free from earth. She knows I am out here in my celestial garden among the stars, embarking on the next adventure, but this doesn't ease her pain.

In the chaos of the airport, I see her falter, the weight of her grief threatening to crush her. She seeks refuge in the ladies' room, but a tidal wave of sorrow overwhelms her. This is the moment she needs help. So I gather the nearby souls whose hearts are open to her pain. I whisper to them, guide them to her side, urge them to offer their strength. They surround her, these kind women; they hold her as she sobs, and their arms offer the comfort she so desperately needs. Their words are filled with love and compassion. I watch as their kindness lifts and carries her through this day and the days that follow.

They didn't know her name, and she didn't know theirs, but their spirits connected in that moment of need. The kindness of strangers made all the difference, and I knew she would not walk this path of grief alone.

"Small acts of kindness can make a BIG difference."
Anonymous

My Advice: Be Kind

by Amy Olmedo

My mom's advice is always short, sweet, and to the point. Her simple wisdom has shaped my life. Like many of her generation, she didn't have a voice. Here is my interpretation:

I was born during the Great Depression, six years after Anne Frank. I graduated high school and moved to the city. There was no future in a small coal mining town. I finished secretarial school before Elvis danced in his blue suede shoes. I met my husband at a church social, although dancing was tough due to his customized polio shoe. Our first daughter was born days before JFK was assassinated. My husband brought coins home from the Space Shuttle Columbia. Anne Murray's love songs still make me cry. All four of my daughters graduated from college. My grandson was born months before 9/11. Mixed family situations are tough. When my husband passed, I lost my best friend. Covid took away my family and my social connections. I was alone. I pray daily to have my girls back together. My family is scattered, and most of my friends have passed. I smile and keep myself busy, but solitude has worn me down. I am not young anymore, but I courageously lived through what you learn from stories.

My Advice: Be kind. Love each other. Stop and smell the roses. Share your light and say hello to that invisible old soul walking the same path. Smile from your heart. You can make a difference in my life. Remember, I am you in a few short years.

"But let the one who boasts boast about this: that they have the understanding to know me, that I am the LORD, who exercises kindness, justice and righteousness on earth, for in these I delight."
Jeremiah 9:24

Kindness and Confidence

by Dr. Beth Goodman

K indness and confidence, though seemingly distinct, are deeply intertwined in my life. I've understood that kindness is an outward expression of compassion and care for others. Still, when it's grounded in inner security, it becomes transformative—not just for those I share it with but also for myself. True confidence, I've discovered, isn't about arrogance or self-importance; it's a quiet assurance that allows me to act gracefully, even in moments of uncertainty.

I remember when I offered a kind word to a stranger. It may seem like a small gesture, but it always takes confidence to step out of my comfort zone, risk vulnerability, and extend kindness without expecting anything in return. This type of kindness, born from confidence, can lift spirits, build connections, and create a ripple effect of positivity.

On the other hand, my confidence flourishes when I practice kindness toward myself. Granting myself grace during times of failure or doubt nurtures an inner strength that helps me show up authentically. This self-kindness and humility have cultivated a resilient confidence that doesn't falter in the face of challenges.

Ultimately, I've realized that kindness and confidence are two sides of the same coin in my life. Confidence allows me to be kind without fear, and kindness, in turn, reinforces my confidence by affirming my values and purpose. Together, they create a cycle of growth that empowers me to impact my community positively.

Let confidence unlock your kindness, and let kindness fuel your confidence. TURN YOUR KEYS!

Where Has All the Kindness Gone?

by Beth Johnston

I s it just me, or do you feel that kindness doesn't flow as abundantly as it once did?

Many seem guarded, almost trying not to be kind as if it were a sign of weakness. What a shame! Kindness should flow naturally. It seems easier to be kind than trying hard not to be!

I'm abundantly blessed to know many very kind people, and the kindest was my Mom, Catherine. Her natural demeanor was gentle, humble, and somewhat meek. She always put the needs of others ahead of her own and never sought recognition nor asked for reciprocal favors. She wore love on her sleeve as seen through her gentle Mona Lisa-like smile. It's almost 30 years since Mom died in my arms (Feb 22nd, 1995.) Her last words were, "I love you." That moment remains her most precious gift of kindness to me, pure love.

Mom visits me regularly through that smile. When I realize someone is smiling at me, I become keenly aware that I am wearing her expression; that's what others are responding to. In those moments, I find my joy explodes and becomes contagious.

What could be easier than smiling at someone? You never know how long it may have been since someone smiled at that person or what your smile might do to brighten their day, to make them feel noticed or valued.

Your smile, or any kindness, might make someone feel like a million bucks; it will make you feel like two!

Be kind: God is watching, and so is your Mom!
Written on Sept 29th, Mom's birthdate, 1922.

THINGS do all With KINDNESS

The Art of Giving

by Cyndi Wilkins

O ne of the most extraordinary contributions we can make to humankind is in service to others. When helping others, we help ourselves, primarily when we aid those who can offer us nothing in return—a selfless act with no expectation of reward.

The reward is feeling good when giving. It makes your heart feel lighter and fills you with joy. That is the art of giving. When multiplied by many, love has the power to change the world.

Small acts of kindness often create remarkable results. A simple pair of gloves, a warm coat, or a hat are significant for a homeless person. Suppose you can afford a small financial donation to an animal shelter, soup kitchen, or even a bit of your time to help care for them.

Shelters are always looking for additional help around the holidays. What a great gift to give yourself, too! It's a very moving experience that fills you with gratitude for your good fortune. A slice of humble pie is good for everyone.

Speaking of slices, I heard an incredible story about a pizza shop owner who began offering a free slice of pizza to the neighborhood homeless every Thursday. Inspired by the shop owner's generosity, his patrons donated money to the cause, and the starving people displayed gratitude.

Now, the pizza shop owner can afford to offer more meals to the hungry several days a week. That's what I call 'awesomeness in action!' People are helping people, one slice at a time. The joy of giving is contagious!

The Gift of a Smile

by Dennis Pitocco

In a world where you can be anything, be kind.
Jennifer Dukes Lee

Many years ago, as I stood at the threshold of adulthood, the world felt both exhilarating and terrifying. Freshly graduated and eager to make my mark, I faced the daunting challenge of finding a job in a competitive market. My heart was heavy with worries about establishing my career and navigating the complexities of adult life. I often found myself lost in thought, barely noticing the vibrant world around me.

One chilly November morning, as I rushed to catch the bus, I spotted a young boy at the stop, clutching a tattered umbrella. His eyes sparkled with anticipation, as if the bus were a magical chariot ready to whisk him away to adventure. Just then, a gust of wind flipped his umbrella inside out, leaving him shivering and exposed. I felt a pang of sympathy but hesitated, too wrapped up in my own concerns to act.

An elderly woman approached. Without a moment's pause, she knelt beside the boy, deftly flipping the umbrella back to its rightful shape.

"There you go, dear," she said. "Now, hold it tight!"

The boy's face lit up, his earlier distress forgotten. His smile brightened the dreary day.

Years later, I reflect on that chilly morning and recognize the profound impact of that small act of kindness. It inspired me to seek opportunities to share kindness in my own life, reminding me that kindness is the most beautiful gift we can give.

God's Love and Kindness
Rises Above Chaos

by Donna Guary

"Do not be overcome by evil, but overcome evil with good."
Romans 12:21

I t was a fall day in 2020, during the unrest following George Floyd's death. The nation was grappling with racial tension, and protests filled the streets. The words Black Lives Matter echoed from coast to coast.

As I left Walmart, I saw an older woman struggling with her car. I asked if I could help and offered to get one of the mechanics to look at her car since the store had an auto repair department. She said she had AAA. Visibly upset, she searched for her card, and we talked easily despite the tension in the world around us.

Once she found the card, she called to ask for assistance. Satisfied that she would be all right, she turned to me and said, "I wish I could hug you." Without hesitation, I replied, "Yes! You can hug me." Amid division, we hugged—a Black woman and an elderly white woman standing in a Walmart parking lot while the country was in turmoil.

In that hug, I felt the power of God's love rising above the chaos. It reminded me that a small act of kindness can pierce through the darkest times. From a heavenly view, perhaps God saw that moment as a beautiful contrast to the division sweeping the nation, a reminder that His love transcends all barriers.

"Be kind, for everyone you meet is fighting a hard battle."
Ian Maclaren (Rev. John Watson)

The Smallest Acts of Kindness Can Lead to Miracles

by Dr. Teresa Lynch

It began with a simple road trip to Virginia Tech. After dropping my daughter off for a fraternity prom, I visited my sister. Feeling drowsy on the way back, I decided to try an audiobook for the first time, randomly choosing *And Then There Were None* by Agatha Christie. The mystery kept me awake, and I made it home safely.

Months later, a close friend called. Her 23-year-old son was battling leukemia, and after losing her husband to cancer, she was desperate for hope. While attending a conference near a specialized hospital, I visited them. At the conference, a researcher shared his groundbreaking work using energy-charged cotton to heal cancer in mice. Thinking of my friend's son, I wondered if it would work for him. I brought a charged piece of cotton filled with love and gave it to him; he placed it in his pillowcase that night.

The following day, something extraordinary happened. My phone randomly opened the audiobook I'd finished months earlier—*And Then There Were None*, Chapter 2. I immediately felt it: "There will be a second chapter in his life!"

A few days later, the doctors confirmed the impossible—his cancer cells were gone. Stunned, they stopped treatment to reevaluate. His cancer never returned.

Sometimes, God answers prayers in ways we can't predict, turning small acts into profound miracles. *And Then There Were None* wasn't just a book; it was a message that a prayer had been answered.

*"To err on the side of kindness is
seldom an error"*
Liz Armbruster

The Lesson of Ollie

by Beth Fitzgerald

Ollie is a yellow lab my daughter Devon and her roommates fostered. When Ollie arrived, he weighed an unhealthy 176 pounds (now 108!). He had been neglected in Mississippi, left outside while kids threw rocks at him. Unsurprisingly, Ollie had challenges—he disliked kids and small dogs and wasn't good on a leash. At his size, he won every tug-of-war. But inside, he was the sweetest dog you could imagine.

After several failed adoption attempts, Ollie finally found his forever home with an amazing woman!

Ollie's story touched me deeply. I wanted him to be adopted so badly, despite his quirks—don't we all have some? I knew the right person was out there. Meanwhile, Devon and her roommates gave Ollie a loving home, and he adored them in return. Everybody deserves that, don't they? To love and be loved.

Ollie made me reflect on how we interact with the world. There are "Ollies" in every part of our lives. If we could look beyond quirks and irritants, we might see the kindness within each person. When you read that "kids threw rocks at Ollie," did it make you sad? Me too. Maybe we should remember that the "Ollies" we meet have likely been hurt, too.

We don't have to agree on everything to be kind. Let's make the world better by showing kindness to everyone, even those with rough edges.

Let's GO! WE GOT THIS!

P.S. To my daughter and her roommates, thank you for your kindness to a soul in need. You're amazing! XO

"Let us be grateful to the people who make us happy;
they are the charming gardeners who make our souls blossom."
Marcel Proust

An Introduction to Kindness

by Sophia Long

My grandfather was the kindest man I ever knew. Between caring for my grandmother and compiling historical binders for his hometown, he made it his mission to fill our lives with fun and love. He rarely drank, quit smoking, and was always mindful of his health, yet had serious heart defects. I cannot recall a time he was truly angry at me or anyone he loved.

Grandpa was always there for us. He took us to our favorite local spots, rented us DVDs, and even brought us along on grocery trips. Sometimes, he let us sleep on his side of the bed so we could have sleepovers with Grandma. He kept drawers full of gag toys, dozens of VCR tapes, and a basement kitchenette stocked with our crafting supplies and toys in his home.

Thoughtfulness came naturally to him, whether you were family or a stranger. One of his last acts of kindness occurred when I graduated from elementary school. My dad had passed away, and my mom, balancing work, could only stay briefly. But Grandpa stayed until the end, ensuring I wouldn't be alone while the other kids ran to their families. Despite his heart defects, he never showed how much pain he must have been in that day, as we lost him a few weeks later.

That memory perfectly captures who my grandfather was—someone who always showed up, no matter what. I hope to carry forward even a fraction of the kindness he extended so freely.

No act of kindness is ever wasted

Spread Kindness Online:
Simple Acts with Big Impact

by Linda B. Kaye

In a world where negativity often fills our social feeds, the importance of digital kindness has never been greater. Acts of kindness, especially during tough times, can change how we see our situation and how we connect with others. When we spread kindness, it creates a positive ripple effect that can touch many lives.

Here are some helpful acronyms to inspire you to take simple acts of online kindness: When we **SHARE** positive words, **SMILE** at someone's achievements, and practice **KINDNESS** through empathy, we can **SPARK** a chain reaction of connection and positivity.

1. S.H.A.R.E. the Love: A Call to Digital Kindness

- **S**upport with kind words
- **H**elp when you can
- **A**cknowledge achievements
- **R**each out to check-in
- **E**ncourage positivity

2. S.M.I.L.E. Often: Simple Steps to Uplift Others Online

- **S**peak kindly
- **M**otivate others
- **I**nclude everyone
- **L**isten actively
- **E**xpress gratitude

3. K.I.N.D.N.E.S.S. Matters: Building Connections in a Digital World

- **K**eep it positive
- **I**nspire others
- **N**urture connections
- **D**emonstrate empathy
- **N**otice when others need support
- **E**ncourage respectful dialogue
- **S**hare positivity
- **S**tay consistent

4. S.P.A.R.K. Change: Igniting Kindness Online

- **S**tart with positivity
- **P**ractice respect
- **A**mplify good deeds
- **R**espond with empathy
- **K**eep the momentum going

Integrating these into your daily online interactions can help foster a more compassionate and caring digital space. Each small effort can significantly change your online community and relationships.

130

Kindness Encounter

by Mark Heidt

*"Wherever there is a human being,
there is an opportunity for kindness."*
Seneca

I was second in line at the checkout counter at Walgreens. In front of me was a very frustrated man because credit cards one, two, and now three were not accepted. In the modern world, I think we all know that feeling. Without judgment, I asked him if he would like me to use my credit card and pay for his items. He replied, "Thank you, but no, I only live a few blocks from here, and I will go and get cash."

After making my purchase, I went to the rear of the store to pick up a prescription from the pharmacy department. On my way out of the store, I again ran into the man from the counter. He went home and returned to the store to pick out his items once again.

Seeing me coming down the aisle, he said, "That was really kind of you. I've never had anyone do something like that for me before. When I have an opportunity to do that kindness for someone else, I'm going to do it."

I said, "That's how we should always be to one another."

Kindness is contagious.

I did not give any thought to my offer before I made it. I just reacted naturally.

Kindness is meant to flow naturally. Let it flow!

Speaking Life:
The Journey of Self-Kindness

by Nicola King

L ove and kindness go hand in hand. When Jesus said, "Love your neighbor as yourself," He wasn't just talking about loving others; He reminded us to be kind to ourselves, too.

Sometimes, we think being kind to ourselves is selfish, but it's actually one of the most generous things we can do so we can love others as commanded. Just like charity begins at home, kindness starts with us.

I realized that to show genuine kindness to others, I needed to start by being kind to myself. What does that mean? It's about treating yourself with the same grace and love that God shows you.

Being kind to yourself means paying attention to how you talk to yourself, your thoughts, and how you care for your body, mind, and soul. It's about celebrating who God made you to be, recognizing your gifts, and letting go of self-criticism. The more you root your identity in Christ, the easier it becomes to show kindness to yourself.

When you're kind to yourself, that kindness overflows into your relationships with others and the world around you.

How can you show kindness to yourself today? Maybe it's by resting, enjoying nature, speaking life over yourself, or simply taking a moment to appreciate who God made you to be.

CH❀❀SE KINDNESS

Full Circle of Kindness: Paying it Forward Twenty Years Later

by Rhonda Douglas Charles

It was an ordinary day at the post office, but for the Haitian small business owner in front of me, it was anything but. He stood at the counter, hands trembling slightly as he tried to send a money order via registered mail to the IRS—a crucial payment. After purchasing the money order, he realized he was five dollars short of the registered mail fee.

He tried two cards, but neither had enough funds. His shoulders slumped in frustration, his face etched with worry. As a small business owner myself, I knew the feeling of stretching every last dollar. At that moment, I saw myself in him. Without thinking, I stepped up and handed the cashier five dollars. It wasn't much, but it allowed him to send his crucial mail.

As I left, I saw him waiting by the door. He thanked me with a smile of relief and gratitude; he even offered me a ride, which I kindly declined. His offer reminded me that kindness is reciprocal.

On the way to my car, a memory surfaced from 20 years ago—on my way to Brooklyn College, I didn't have enough change for the bus. A stranger stepped in and paid for me. That small act lifted a weight off my shoulders, much like I hoped to do for him today.

Now, years later, I realize kindness has come full circle. It's a reminder that even the smallest acts of compassion can ripple through time, returning to us when we least expect it.

Shine Your Light

by Renea Attaway

D aily, a random act of kindness is a beautiful gift that brings hope to hurting people. In a world filled with darkness and evil, it is delightful to see young people blessing others with daily gifts of kindness. Recently, I encountered a young hairstylist who spends one of her days off volunteering at a Center of Hope— a ministry that gives homeless people a place for a meal, bath, laundry, and a haircut. This 19-year-old raised donations to help furnish a salon for people experiencing homelessness at this ministry. She is a blessing and shows the love and compassion of the Heavenly Father.

Soon after that, I was blessed to receive a gift of kindness from a young man who was a complete stranger. I was in a Dollar Tree picking up some Items for a Vision Board when the young man in front of me asked the cashier to add my items to his bill. I was quite taken aback and blessed at the same time. I almost refused, but the Lord prompted me not to keep him from his blessing. So, I thanked him and prayed a blessing over him. I wonder how much light we can shine on the darkness and what joy others could experience if we all gave a gift of kindness daily. I challenge you to make a daily effort to let your light shine through purposeful kindness to others.

"What wisdom can you find that is greater than kindness?"
Jean-Jacques Rousseau

The Day the Rain Came

by Dr. Kate Keville

My son has sponsored orphans around the world for many years. In 2017, he was invited to Uganda to meet the families he'd supported with books, education, food, and clothing. He asked me to join him on this three-week journey into the Ugandan bush.

When we arrived, we learned the country had been in a drought for months. Clean water was a rare and precious resource due to contaminated water sources, and now the lack of rain was compounding the hardship.

One morning, as we visited a family in the bush, a member of the household learned I was a holistic doctor and asked if I could help a mother who had been suffering ever since a coconut tree had fallen on her head three years before. She was bedridden most days, plagued by severe headaches and neck pain.

With nowhere else to sit, I had her perch on a tree stump. I examined her, identified the source of the pain, and carefully performed an adjustment to her upper cervical spine. As soon as the adjustment was complete, her eyes opened wide, filling with tears. "No pain," she whispered in disbelief.

Then, as if in response, it began to rain. People poured out of their homes, arms lifted, voices proclaiming, "It's raining!" In their culture, rain arriving in a time of need is a miracle.

Was it the woman's healing that brought the rain that day in the Ugandan bush? We'll never know for sure. But witnessing that moment, seeing lives touched and renewed, changed us forever.

"Therefore, as God's chosen people, holy and dearly loved clothe yourselves with compassion, kindness, humility, gentleness and patience.
Colossians 3:12

Kindness Has a Genetic Expression

Dr. Rachelle Simpson-Sweet

S tella had always been fascinated by the idea that emotions could affect the world around us. She once read how water molecules change their structure when exposed to positive versus negative energy. Kindness and love created beautiful, harmonious shapes, while anger and fear produced chaotic, disjointed ones. This idea stayed with her, but she never imagined something similar could happen inside her body until a conversation about genetics changed her perspective.

"Kindness doesn't just make us feel good," a friend shared. "It can change the way our genes express themselves."

Stella had never thought of kindness as healing before. As she continued to provide meals and supplies for those in need, she felt a profound shift in her mood and overall health. She didn't realize that, much like the shapes in water, her kind actions were helping to reshape her internal environment.

Kindness lowers stress hormones like cortisol, which, in turn, boosts the immune system. It also triggers the release of oxytocin, the "love hormone," which promotes healing and resilience. Scientists are discovering that these shifts can influence gene expression, creating a ripple effect that strengthens both body and mind. Kindness was, quite literally, reshaping Stella from the inside out—fostering not just emotional well-being but physical health, too.

As Stella reflected on this, she marveled at the idea that something as simple as kindness could nurture both her spirit and her genes, helping her become more resistant to the stresses of life. Learning about her genetics guided her toward a life filled with more balance, resilience, vitality, and kindness.

"Kindness is the golden chain by which society is bound together."
Johann Wolfgang von Goethe

A Gift of Kindness: A Christmas to Remember

by Jodie Fitzgerald

When I was a young single mother, going to school to complete my high school degree, I lived with my nine-month-old daughter in a low-rental apartment.

One wintery December day, there was a knock on my door. I opened it and saw a man standing there with a young boy by his side. The man held a large box in his arms. He handed it to me with a cheerful "Merry Christmas."

I had just received a Christmas hamper!

I was brought to tears immediately. Inside this basket was a turkey and some food, and there were two beautiful gifts for my daughter—a little pair of yellow-knitted mittens and an adorable children's book.

Thirty-seven years later, I can still remember this heartwarming event and feel the love from this amazing gift of kindness.

Kind Words CAN HEAL Deep WOUNDS

I Choose Kindness

by Sally Mary S. de Leon

T he world is a symphony of joy and sorrow, love and loss, each note resonating with the human experience. Amidst this ever-changing melody, I'm drawn to the enduring power of kindness—a steadfast flame burning even in the deepest darkness. It's not grand or fleeting but a quiet echo of the soul, a gentle touch mending the fractures within us.

Kindness is not a grand performance but a quiet echo of the soul that can transform the harshest landscapes into fertile ground for hope. I've seen it in a child offering a hand to a fallen friend, in the embrace of a loved one offering solace in grief, and strangers reaching out with open hearts. These moments remind us of the inherent goodness within us all.

But, oh, the sting of tears when kindness meets indifference, an outstretched hand is met with a closed fist, and a gentle voice is drowned out by a world that has forgotten how to listen. In those moments, the heart aches for the lost opportunities to connect, heal, and love.

Yet even in sorrow, kindness persists. The unwavering ember refuses to be extinguished, the quiet reminder of our shared humanity. A single act of kindness can illuminate a brighter tomorrow.

So, I choose kindness—a source of light and warmth, a steady hand reaching out to those lost and alone. It is the redeeming power of love and enduring hope in a world that can seem cold and unforgiving.

Looking at Kindness from Both Sides

by Mary Vovers Brown

Kindness blooms in hearts that care
In every smile and every stare
Nurturing souls with gentle grace
Delivering warmth in every space
Never fleeting, always near
Echoing love, dispelling fear
Small gestures bring light we all can share
Spreading hope, with kindness, there

A gentle touch can break the darK
A word of care can hit the mark. You see, I
Believe we should have it dowN
With simple steps, our hearts unbounD
The smallest act can ease a paiN
In kindness, we find love won't wanE
It's through these acts we find succesS
So let us give and share our light, no lesS

Whichever way you look at it, a little **KINDNESS** goes a long way.

Blessings
ARE THE HARVEST OF
KINDNESS

Just Pay it Forward

by BJ Largent

I was sitting at my surgeon's desk as they explained my bill, which was far more than I had anticipated. Tears welled up as I asked if I could be put on a payment plan. As I waited for their response, my mind raced with anxious thoughts—Which bill can I skip? Could I purposely send a check in the wrong envelope? Who could I possibly borrow money from?

While I waited, I tried to wipe away my tears discreetly. Then, out of nowhere, I heard a woman's voice say, "Please put $200 from my card on her account." I couldn't believe what I was hearing.

I looked up to see a woman, large in stature and spirit, smiling at me with the warmest smile I'd ever seen.

"Oh my, how will I ever thank you?" I asked, overwhelmed by her generosity.

"There's no need," she replied. "Just pay it forward."

I asked if I could get her name and address (I firmly believe in sending thank-you cards).

"My name is Penny Bliss," she said.

I was speechless. Bliss. She was exactly that to me in that moment—pure bliss. That day, Penny Bliss taught me the profound importance of paying it forward, a lesson I carry with me and try to honor every chance I get.

Penny Bliss showed me that miracles happen when you least expect them. There are good people everywhere, and it's our responsibility to pass kindness on whenever we can. I'll never forget the moment Penny Bliss entered my life to teach me this lesson, and I hope you also take this story to heart.

Please pay it forward. It truly makes a difference.

In A World Where You Can Be Anything

Be Kind

A Christmas Miracle

by Jane Caponigro

My son was in his very demanding junior year at college, thirteen hours away from home. He was looking forward to getting home for winter break. I asked him not leave at night, stressing my concern for winter weather road conditions, but he insisted he would be alright.

He began driving around 8pm. I fell asleep and didn't hear the phone ring at midnight. When I called him back, his first words were, "Mom I am alright." I was so scared, my heart felt like it fell out of my chest. He slid on black ice into a ditch in Ohio 7.5 hours away from home. Hearing the fear in his voice, all I wanted to do was to hug him tightly.

He was talking to the Deputy Sheriff about his classes and where he worked as an intern over the summer, while they figured out where to tow the car, which was full of computers, a 3D printer, and of course, his laundry.

They towed it to a reputable body shop. The Deputy Sheriff even paid for a hotel for my son. "Keep up the good work and send me a copy of your grades and we'll call it even," he said.

I arrived about 10 AM. We went to the body shop. Although it could have taken a few weeks to repair, they got the parts and made the repair right away. We headed home that day at 3 PM.

The kindness of the people who helped him made a Christmas Miracle happen for our family.

"Kindness is free. Sprinkle that stuff everywhere."
Anonymous

Always Put Others First

by Lucia Murphy

Growing up, I was into local bands and supporting local businesses because they are nothing like corporations that are around forever. My Mom and Dad came to this country from Italy in 1966 with nothing more than the clothing on their backs. They worked until they opened their pizza shop, Lucia's Pizza, in downtown Scranton in 1979 to support my brother and me. My dad passed when I was very young, and I am thankful we still have my mother.

Years ago, I started a website called OneWay2Fun. I listed businesses on the website and supported them however I could. This was just the beginning of being able to give back.

I expanded this endeavor onto social media, and now my husband and I have a very successful YouTube channel. We have created a following and a great social media family when it comes to dining out or traveling somewhere. We get a lot of suggestions daily, so we are always deciding where to go next.

We do this so that people can follow us, living vicariously through us, and so that we can have fun living our best lives.

I have become a kind-hearted giver, not a taker, because God and my dad would want it that way. So now I give back to the public as much as possible through my business, Autobahn Title & Tag, helping those who can't afford notary services.

"Whoever is generous to the poor lends to the Lord, and he will repay him for his deed."
Proverbs 19:17

The Energy of Kindness

by Markus Wettstein

My childhood was marred with physical violence in the home. As a result, I learned to identify upcoming trouble early. In fact, I appear to have a stress response which is quite pronounced. Even small issues cause my throat to tighten, my heart to race, and my stomach to tie into knots. I found ways to avoid intense situations. Early on, this entailed guessing what people wanted and providing it before they asked.

Now, I revise my social interaction whenever I can remember to do so.

Firstly, do I really want to do something kind for someone else? If it feels like an obligation, it sends out negative energies that are easily picked up by others. Sometimes, the incentive of not having to stare at a laundry pile is enough for me to fold the laundry for my wife. It results in an overall positive experience, despite the obligation.

Secondly, is the receiver of this kindness ready? Most people feel obligated to return the favor. They turn grumpy due to the perceived burden of a future obligation. In those situations, positive energy is expressed with kindness, but negative energy comes back. As a result, there is a poor outcome.

Thirdly, is the receiver an energy vampire? As expectations of kindness arise, setting limits becomes critical. Once there are expectations of kind behavior, it does not create external happiness anymore.

So, kindness must be free from expectations or negativity to be sincere. In other words, kindness must come from the heart.

"Do things for people not because of who they are or what they do in return, but because of who you are."
Rabbi Harold S. Kushner

Live Life Live

by Mick Vovers

Thumbs up to the real folks, who live their lives live,
We all start from the same place and all will arrive
At that full stop, that instant, when our body is laid.
Your soul is your impact, so what have you made?

We all learn to eat, learn to dress, learn how to walk.
It's no curious thing that most of us can talk.
It's a difficult task, that most parents do
Then you're out on your own kid, and it's all up to you

And thumbs up to the good folks who live their lives live

The more you do, see and hear, the more you can feel
Not from some silly screen but out here for real
We are each the sum total of every shred
Of light, sound and rumor that has entered our head

And thumbs up to the good folks who live their lives live

It's your choice, it's your life, you are what you eat,
But you'll never find magic if you're stuck on repeat,
No door will be opened if you don't go and knock,
Every moment is precious, we're all on the clock,

And thumbs up to the good folks who live their lives live

Turn off your phones, get together, get up here and dance

My stories are real and ongoing, I'm not here by chance
Fill your life with real action, before you arrive
At that same end, with us real folks, who live their lives live.

In 2023, Mick Vovers created a painting of his musician friend Katie called "Live Life Live." Over the six months he was at the easel, this song emerged to accompany it.

If you would like to see Mick singing it on April 14, 2024, find it on Facebook here:
https://www.facebook.com/share/p/ixwzjAwdpB5vw6F8/

A Gift of Kindness Gone Awry

by Dr. Teresa Lynch

O n a crisp March afternoon, my middle-school-aged son, Sean, approached me. "Mom, you've taken Katherine to many plays, but I've never been to one." His younger sister had enjoyed several outings, but as the second of four children, Sean often felt overlooked.

I smiled. "We'll make it happen."

Soon after, my sister-in-law called. "We have extra tickets to *Chitty Chitty Bang Bang.* Could you use them?" Thrilled, I accepted, knowing Sean would finally get his chance.

To make the day even more special, we prepared a lunch for a homeless person. Sean, his siblings, and I decorated a bag and filled it with a turkey sandwich, an apple, and cookies. Excited, we set off into the busy streets of New York, determined to find someone in need.

Near the New York Public Library, we spotted a man in a wheelchair holding a sign: "Blind. Need money." Sean bravely approached him. "Sir, we made a lunch for you."

The man frowned. "Kid, did you read the sign? I need money, not food."

Deflated, Sean returned. "Mom, I thought you said beggars can't be choosers."

I sighed. "Apparently, they can, Sean. Apparently, they can."

That day, we learned that kindness is about giving without expectations. Genuine kindness allows others the freedom to accept or decline without judgment.

And by the way, Sean makes a delicious turkey sandwich!

KIND WORDS ARE LIKE HONEY
sweet to the soul
PROVERBS 16:24

In His Image©

by Laurie Hilton Rowland (1986)

I look into the mirror; your face I wish I'd see.
Instead I stand there staring at the same pathetic me.
The me too weak and feeble to resist the tempter's spoil.
Too proud to be called humble; too hard to be soft soil.
Amazed to be called chosen, I'm baffled by your choice.
So often earthly pleasures drown out your still small voice.
I grope my way through darkness, forgetting you're the light.
Defeated and discouraged, I long to do what's right.
Then looking to your word, your scripture pierces through;
Like thunder breaking silence, I'm reminded of what's true.
That Jesus lives and dwells within; His blood has set me free.
When you look into my mirror, it's the you in me you see.

Listen to the recording. Sung by Casey Kearny
https://youtu.be/7U6nGYvMhus?si=u2oAGIGstXPULyia

Always

BE★KIND

Afterword
The Kindness of Being Yourself

by Martariesa Logue

F rom the moment you learned you were expecting me, your love was overwhelming and unshakeable. Despite doctors' discouraging prognosis—urging ermination due to concerns over potential retardation and physical deformities—you chose to embrace the challenge. Your heart was resolute, guided by an unbreakable faith in the potential of the tiny life growing within you.

Throughout the trials and heartbreaks that followed, your compassion was never compromised. You faced each difficulty gracefully, determined to protect me - even from your fears and struggles. Your kindness was your strength; you encouraged me with every fiber of your being.

You went above and beyond to ensure my and my sister's well-being. You tirelessly volunteered for school events and community activities, fighting for fair treatment and creating opportunities. Your love overflowed in every action—taking me to Sunday school, introducing me to God's love, and teaching me to cherish life's every moment with compassion and joy.

Even while managing your own health challenges, you wore a constant, encouraging smile. Your resilience and kindness crafted an environment where I felt supported and empowered to pursue my dreams. Your selfless dedication and boundless love were evident in every aspect of our lives.

At the same time, Dad worked (and still works) tirelessly to provide for the family, allowing you to focus entirely on my and my sister's upbringing. His support was indispensable; together, you built a home brimming with love, kindness, and encouragement. I flourished in this nurturing environment, inspired by the extraordinary kindness and selflessness you showed, ready to approach life with the same heartwarming spirit.

The first thing I need to say to you is thank you. These two words are said so often in our household that they sometimes lose meaning. This isn't the kind of "thank you" you say when someone gives you the last cookie or holds the door open for you. This kind of "thank you" means something much deeper. Thank you for making me laugh so hard that I cry and laugh when I cry. Thank you for loving me and my flaws but for not allowing that love to hide my flaws. Thank you for making my life difficult sometimes. In full swing of those "sometimes," I was bitter, angry, and confused, but looking back as a stronger, gentler, and more focused woman, now I say "thank you."

Thank you for not allowing me to get everything that I wanted. Thank you for making me work for my first cell phone. Thank you for making me work for your respect. Thank you for making me re-write an essay because you knew it could be better. Thank you for making me go the extra mile. Because of you, I now find joy in doing these things that once caused so much drama. Thank you because I finally feel like I am slowly becoming more and more like you, who God gave as an example of someone striving to be more and more like Christ.

The second, but probably (no, most definitely) the most important thing I need you to understand is that I love you. These three words are thrown around like a football, and with every careless pass, they are intercepted by doubt. But not these words: I love you. I know I don't call you to tell you that enough, but I do. Sometimes, while lying in bed at night mulling over the events of that day, I think of you. Sometimes, I lie in bed smiling because I think of something you said or did.

Finally, I want you to know that I am proud of you. I know it's your job to be proud of me, and I know you are. Now, it's my turn. I am so proud to be called your daughter. I am beyond proud of how hard you have worked being a mom, an aunt, a cousin, and a friend. With courage, perseverance, dedication, and flat-out hard work, you raised a family. You are the best nurse who has ever cared for me, who always knows exactly what's wrong. With your fingertips on my forehead, you know my temperature and what would make me feel better. You are the best counselor who listens to every word and responds with love-based but stern words of encouragement and direction. You are my best cheerleader. You were on the sidelines of every game, cheered louder than anyone, and always had a special way of motivating and encouraging me. You will always be better than any coach (sorry, not sorry, Coach). I'm proud, probably more than you realize, of the impact you have in the lives of many. I am proud of you, Tammy, aka Mom.

Your never-ending kindness and love have been my guiding light, after Jesus, of course. You have helped me overcome life's challenges, especially those that come from living with TAR Syndrome. Your constant encouragement has made all the difference despite the physical and emotional struggles. Your compassion has shown me that my limitations do not define me, but by the strength and love you have instilled in me.

This story is dedicated to all mothers who face incredible challenges with unwavering kindness and love. Your dedication makes a world of difference from a daughter's perspective. May you be encouraged by my story and inspired to continue showing love and encouragement to your children, for it shapes their lives in the most profound ways.

To learn more about my story, see "A Daily Gift of Hope," where I talk about TAR Syndrome.

What is World Kindness Day?
World Kindness Day: A Global Celebration of Humanity

Compiled by Mary Vovers Brown

O bserved annually on November 13, World Kindness Day was established in 1998 by the World Kindness Movement (WKM) to promote acts of kindness around the world. Celebrated across many countries, this day highlights the simple yet profound power of kindness to connect people from all walks of life.

The theme for 2024 is *Make Kindness the Standard, Not the Exception,* with communities globally marking the day in creative ways.

It's well-documented that acts of kindness, whether small or large, can significantly uplift the well-being of both the giver and the receiver. A study published in the Journal of Social Psychology explored the effects of performing five acts of kindness per week over six weeks. The results showed a marked increase in happiness for participants, with the positive effects lasting up to three months. Kindness strengthens social connections, fosters empathy, and shifts focus away from personal stress or negativity. It even triggers a "helper's high," releasing dopamine and other feel-good chemicals. By regularly practicing kindness, we can experience lasting improvements in our well-being.

In Australia, World Kindness Day became part of the New South Wales school calendar in 2010, and by 2012, it was recognized nationally, impacting over 9,000 schools. Several councils, representing more than 1.3 million Australians, also support this movement. Schools worldwide now celebrate World Kindness Day annually.

In the UK, David Jamilly co-founded Kindness Day UK with Louise Burfitt-Dons. It's embraced by charities, businesses, schools, and organizations across the nation. The School of Kindness, part of the 52

Lives charity, offers free Kindness Workshops, resources, and lesson plans. On November 13, they hold World Kindness Day Virtual Assemblies for primary schools. Last year, over 71,000 children participated, with an even larger event planned for 2024. The 52 Lives charity aims to change a life every week of the year, ensuring 100% of donations go directly to those in need. So far, they've positively impacted 454 lives. Learn more at 52-lives.org.

In Singapore, 45,000 yellow flowers were given away on World Kindness Day in 2009, brightening the streets and bringing smiles to thousands.

In the U.S., The Be Kind People Project in Scottsdale, Arizona, challenges schools to take the "Be Kind" pledge, creating a culture of kindness in classrooms. The project reaches all 50 states, 10 countries, and 3,736 cities globally. Learn more at thebekindpeopleproject.org.

In New York City, Life Vest Inside (LVI) is dedicated to inspiring and educating people to lead a life of kindness. In 2011, they gained widespread attention with their video Kindness Boomerang, set to the Matisyahu song "One Day," which showcases the ripple effect of a single act of kindness. In 2012, LVI launched the annual Dance For Kindness event, where participants from around the world join in a synchronized Freeze/Flashmob. The 10th Annual Dance for Kindness took place in 2022. Find out more at danceforkindness.com.

In Greece, children organized The Big Hug as part of a kindness campaign, and in 2018, the Kappa Sigma Fraternity helped break the record for the largest hug in the United States during the event.

How Can You Celebrate World Kindness Day?

Get creative and imaginative. Kindness costs nothing but its impact can be priceless. Here are some ideas to get you started:

- **Kindness Rocks:** Paint small rocks with positive messages and hide them in parks and public spaces for others to find.

- **Scavenger Hunt:** Create a list of kind acts for your group to complete, then share your experiences at the end of the day.
- **Random Acts of Kindness (RAKs):** Consciously perform a dozen random acts of kindness on November 13—both for people you know and for strangers.
- **Bully A Plant:** Watch and share IKEA's Bully A Plant video, which shows the effect of positive vs. negative words on plants. Use this as inspiration to spread kindness to plants and people alike!
- **Dance of Kindness:** Organize a Freeze/Flashmob in your community for World Kindness Day.
- **Visit the Elderly:** Spend time with elderly people in your community, whether for a chat or to help with daily tasks.
- **Plan for RAK Day:** Start preparing 12 more acts of kindness for Random Acts of Kindness Day on February 17. Involve your family, friends, and neighbors.

Remember to capture the joy of the day by taking photos and tagging @inspirekindacts or using the hashtag #worldkindnessday.

From gifting flowers in Singapore to organizing global flash mobs, World Kindness Day reminds us that kindness is essential to our shared humanity. It breaks down barriers, fosters understanding, and unites people across the globe. Let's work together to make kindness the norm, not the exception.

This information was sourced from:

Wikipedia - World Kindness Day
   https://en.wikipedia.org/wiki/World_Kindness_Day
World Kindness Movement - We Are Kinder National Today
   https://www.theworldkindnessmovement.org/the-world-kindness-movement
National Today
   https://nationaltoday.com/world-kindness-day
Inspire Kindness
   https://inspirekindness.com/blog/world-kindness-day-your-complete-guide
The Random Acts of Kindness Foundation
   https://www.randomactsofkindness.org/world-kindness-day

Resources for Parents, Teachers and Kindness Ambassadors

- **World Kindness Movement** A global organization that unites countries and organizations around the common goal of promoting kindness and compassion globally. They aim to create a kinder world by collaborating across borders. www.theworldkindnessmovement.org
- **Kindness.org** Blending the power of research with the heart of kindness, Kindness.org inspires people to take small, impactful steps towards kindness. Through their Kindlab, they explore the science behind positive behaviors, developing tools and programs that empower us all to choose kindness every day. www.kindness.org
- **Greater Good Science Center (GGSC) at UC Berkeley** The GGSC offers science-based insights and resources on kindness, empathy, and social- emotional learning. They provide parents and teachers with research-backed practices for fostering compassion, resilience, and emotional well-being in children. www.ggsc.berkeley.edu
- **Character.org** Supporting parents and educators in fostering a culture of kindness and ethical values in schools and homes. They provide tools, guides, and certification programs to help develop character and promote positive behavior in children. www.character.org
- **Life Vest Inside** A movement dedicated to empowering individuals to spread kindness, fostering a global community of compassionate change-makers. Through inspirational videos, social campaigns, and grassroots events, Life Vest Inside makes waves of positivity felt across the world because "it's kindness that keeps the world afloat". Social Emotional Learning curriculum, newsletters, www.lifevestinside.com

- **Kindness Curriculum** A unique Social Emotional Learning curriculum designed to easily implement the themes of kindness, compassion and empathy directly into existing school curricula. With one unit of study for grades K-5, each unit is made up of 6 lessons, one building on the next. www.lifevestinside.com/kindness-curriculum
- **Kindness Newsletters from Life Vest Inside**

  - **The Daily Kind** Sent out Monday through Friday. A 30-second read that contains an act of kindness, inspirational quote, positive affirmation and kindness media.
  - **Kindness Flash** Sent out once a month, this 5-minute read includes Thoughts, Songs, Stories, Books, Pictures and Questions centered around Kindness. Join the Kindness Revolution and help build a kinder world. www.lifevestinside.com/kindness-newsletters

- **Dance For Kindness** Life Vest Inside's signature event. Join thousands around the world united under the banner of kindness and take part in a worldwide FlashMob to the same song, same dance all on the same day. Dance for Kindness has taken place in over 310 cities, spanning across 76 countries and 6 continents with over 90,000 GLOBAL participants. www.danceforkindness.com
- **Project Hope Exchange** A Life Vest Inside and Adversity 2 Advocacy joint initiative. Making 30 seconds count. Listen to a message of hope or record your very own 30 second anonymous message; giving hope to others battling an adversity you've faced or are currently facing. When we GIVE HOPE we GET HOPE. Call the Hope Line 1-855-975-HOPE (4673) or visit www.projecthopeexchange.com

- **The A2A Alliance leading the way from Adversity to Alliance** A2A is creating the world's largest network of individuals who have successfully turned a personal challenge into service to others with similar challenges. At the core of A2A's mission is a commitment to showcasing the experiential AND empirical evidence supporting the age-old adage that we help ourselves by helping others. https://a2aalliance.org

- **The Kind Campaign** Focused on promoting kindness among young people, especially girls, The Kind Campaign addresses bullying through school assemblies, educational programs, and online resources. They empower students to foster positive interactions and build a culture of kindness. www.kindcampaign.com

- **Kindness UK** Promoting kindness in schools, workplaces, and communities across the UK, this organization is on a mission to infuse every aspect of British life with empathy, understanding, and connection. www.secondstep.org

- **Kindness Matters** Dedicated to showing how acts of kindness can change the world, this initiative raises awareness about the profound impact of positive actions. Through stories and resources, they inspire individuals to make kindness a daily habit. www.kindnessmatters.co

- **Spreading Kindness Campaign** A community-driven effort based in Eugene and Springfield, Oregon, creating a culture of kindness from the ground up. Through local initiatives, they bring people together to spread kindness daily. www.spreadingkindnesscampaign.org

- **Compassion It** Inspiring kindness through action! Compassion It encourages compassionate living through education and simple reminders— wearable symbols—to keep empathy at the forefront of everyday life. www.compassionit.com

- **The Smile Foundation** Empowering underprivileged children in India through education, healthcare, and livelihood programs. The Smile Foundation infuses their work with kindness, providing opportunities for a brighter, more compassionate future. www.smilefoundationindia.org
- **Kindness To Action** Founded in memory of Elijah James Knight, this initiative turns grief into a mission for kindness. Their unique Kindness Coins track acts of kindness across the globe, sharing stories that inspire others to carry Elijah's message: "Start everything with kindness and the end will be okay." www.kindnesstoaction.org
- **Growing Kindness Project** Spreading kindness one bloom at a time! By growing and gifting flowers, this project connects communities and fosters meaningful interactions. They offer resources to help you garden with a purpose. www.growingkindnessproject.org
- **The Honey Foundation** Buzzing with positivity, The Honey Foundation inspires kindness through education and their "Deed Feed," where good deeds are celebrated. Their "Bee Kind" events encourage communities to spread kindness far and wide. www.honeyfoundation.org
- **EmpathyLab UK** EmpathyLab is dedicated to inspiring children to build a more empathetic world through books. They provide resources for parents and educators, including empathy-building activities, booklists, and training on how to integrate empathy into reading practices. www.empathylab.uk
- **Spread Kindness** "Share a Smile. Be Kind. Pass it On." This initiative provides tools and projects to inspire kind actions, reminding us that a little kindness goes a long way. www.spreadkindness.org

- **Kindness at Ohio State University** Fostering a culture of kindness on campus, Ohio State University's kindness initiatives empower students to spread positivity throughout their community. www.kind.osu.edu
- **Random Acts of Kindness Foundation (RAK)** Celebrating the big impact of small gestures, RAK encourages kindness through resources, inspiring stories, and the message that simple acts can make the world a better place. www.randomactsofkindness.org
- **Learning for Justice (was Teaching Tolerance)** This project by the Southern Poverty Law Center offers free resources for educators to teach respect, kindness, and inclusivity in classrooms. They provide lesson plans, articles, and webinars to create an environment where every student feels respected. www.learningforjustice.org
- **Playworks** focuses on creating positive school environments through play and physical activity. Their programs encourage kindness, inclusivity, and conflict resolution during recess and throughout the school day, offering tools for teachers and parents to support positive play. www.playworks.org
- **Good Deeds Day** What started in Israel has become a global movement that unites people in over 108 countries. Good Deeds Day encourages everyone to take a moment to do something kind, creating a ripple effect of positivity and community spirit. www.good-deeds-day.org
- **Doing Good Together** DGT's mission is to empower families to raise children who care and contribute. Explore a range of creative ebooks, book lists, and compassion-building activity kits to help organizations and big- hearted families promote kindness. Doing Good Together is celebrating its 20th Anniversary in 2024. www.doinggoodtogether.org

- **Second Step** A widely used social-emotional learning (SEL) program, Second Step offers curricula that teach skills like empathy, kindness, and problem-solving to children from early learning through high school. It's designed for educators but also offers tools that parents can use at home. www.secondstep.org
- **The Be Kind People Project** Transforming school culture with the power of kindness! Their "Be Kind Pledge" teaches essential skills of kindness, creating a positive impact in schools and beyond, reaching 10 countries and thousands of communities worldwide. www.thebekindpeopleproject.org

Front Cover
Contributing Authors

Alysia Lyons is a Master Neuro-transformation Results Coach, Mom Support Coach, author and a Podcast host. As the proud mother of a son who has been her own course corrector, she now leads parents through long-lasting neurological shifts to help ease their guilt and increase their emotional peace to find their happy.

Alyssa Ruge is an award-winning attorney with over 20 years of public and private experience. She is admitted before the Supreme Court of the United States and the Florida Bar to practice law. Alyssa graduated from Stetson University College of Law in 2003 with her Juris Doctor, where she was a member of the Stetson Law Review. She is also a graduate of the University of South Florida, where she obtained her Bachelor of Arts degree in Political Science in 2001. She recently became a licensed foster parent in Florida and encourages others to become foster parents.

Amanda Beth Johnson is an intuitive energy healer, and best-selling author committed to helping individuals embrace transformation and self-discovery. Based in Southeast Iowa, she uses ThetaHealing to guide clients in releasing limiting beliefs, fostering personal growth, and serving clients globally. Her journey inspired her to write *Blooming into Life*, sharing insights on overcoming challenges and finding authentic empowerment. With a unique blend of healing services and passions for classic cars, gardening, and crochet, Amanda brings a multifaceted approach to holistic well-being. Join her in exploring the path to fulfillment and transformation in all aspects of life.

Amy Olmedo is on a mission from God. Her first goal is to publish *White Heron: A Creation Story*, a blend of spirituality, mythology, and life lessons that inspire triumph over tragedy. Explore her journey by purchasing the book, visiting her website, and joining her community at www.whiteheron.us.

Amy's second goal is to create a retreat where nature becomes a sanctuary for healing and self-discovery. Amidst mystical woodland trails and a honey bee farm, guests can rest, reconcile the past, and recreate their future, embracing the transformative power of nature and inner wisdom.

Andi Buerger, JD is the founder of Voices Against Trafficking and a survivor, author, and advocate for victims worldwide. Her books, *Voices Against Trafficking - The Strength of Many Voices Speaking As One* and *A Fragile Thread of Hope: One Survivor's Quest to Rescue*, are available on Amazon.com as well as her Voices Of Courage magazine. Andi's new release debuts in 2025 along with a television program also titled Voices of Courage. Her work continues to appear in numerous magazines and books such as *Unsheltered: Voices from the Street* by Peggy Willms and Dennis Pitocco and the best-selling compilation, *Wellness G.P.S*

Chantay Bridges is a powerhouse in business and publishing, founder of Bridges Publishing House, accomplished author, Realtor, speaker, and dedicated philanthropist. Recognized by the White House and local officials, she's collaborated with numerous VIPs, celebrities, presidents, and dignitaries. Chantay's extensive expertise and strong business acumen make her the professional you want to hire. Her impressive  work ethic and commitment have earned her numerous awards and media attention. She's been featured in prestigious outlets such as USA Today, Wall Street Journal, Forbes, and Architectural Digest. As a Christian and respected public figure, Chantay exemplifies excellence and delivers outstanding results.

Fran Asaro is a YouTube Mentor and Strategist. She is the Founder of the Senior Tuber Community where she helps mature people become well-versed YouTube Content creators as she walks them through the steps to leave their legacy, earn additional income, and share their gifts with the world. For more info visit: https://services.seniortuber.com/allservices or https://services.seniortuber.com/senior-tuber-circle

Givonna Cheeks, Ph.D., PMP, CBCP, serves as President/CEO of Entero Emergency Management Consulting, INC. (DBA Entero Solutions). Givonna earned a Ph.D. from Capella University where she studied Public Safety Leadership with a concentration in Emergency Management. Before attending Capella University, she earned a Master of Science in Business Management from Troy State University.  Givonna has proudly served for 22 ½ years in the United States Army with two combat tours in Iraq and Afghanistan. Through numerous military and civilian leadership experiences, Givonna has learned exemplary leadership and genuine care and concern are vital to sustained organization growth and success.

Ida Ra Nalbandian is a former university lecturer who taught philology, linguistics, and comparative literature. She is the author of multiple books, including Does God Have a Bicycle, and Jacob's Magic Vegetables: How Loving Kindness Grows. In addition, she is a contributing author to A Daily Gift of Hope: A Collection of Stories from Hopeful Hearts Around the Globe, and Portals. Energetic Doorways to Mystical Experiences Between Worlds (with Freddy Silva) Ida and her family founded VSCF-Vahagn Setian Charitable Foundation in memory of her late son, whose life was tragically cut short by a drunk driver. Ida honors the foundation's mission of promoting self-awareness, attentive choices, and the expansion of the greater good. (see www.vahagn foundation.org). https://vahagnfoundation.org

Ilene Gottlieb is The Heart Healer. She's been in nursing for over 50 years, with 30 years in Vibrational Healing. Ilene is an expert in creating and using holistic approaches to clear energy blocks and promote healing. She helps an International clientele of heart-centered individuals and entrepreneurs who struggle with trauma, fear, self-sabotaging negative thoughts or behaviors, and self-worth issues. Working with Ilene, her clients experience inner peace, self-confidence, empowerment, and a knowing of their soul's purpose. Ilene has served 1,000s of clients globally as an International Speaker and Vibrational Healer. She is the Founder of The Heart Healers Ho'oponopono Community.
https://linktr.ee/ilenegottlieb.thehearthealer

January Liddell a dedicated financial professional with over three years of experience, helps clients achieve tax-free gains and financial security through her ERFT method: "Eliminating Risk, Fees, and Taxes." Guided by Christian values, January protects her clients' hard-earned money from market volatility, ensuring peace of mind and long-term success. She is the author of *Alina, The Super Saver*, and co-host of the Sexy Freedom Media Podcast. Married to a retired veteran and mother of two, January enjoys boogie boarding, archery, and church. Her positive energy, financial expertise, and unwavering commitment make her a trusted ally in financial planning. Learn more at: www.januaryliddell.com.

Dr. Kate Keville's diverse career includes serving in U.S. Army Military Intelligence and owning four vegetarian restaurants. With a B.S. in Education and a Doctorate in Chiropractic, she's an avid athlete and experienced in healthcare modalities such as Cranio-Sacral Therapy, Myofascial Release, acupuncture, and nutrition. Her mission is to educate people on optimal health. Dr. Kate has developed The Shift Device, a  tool enhancing the body's electromagnetic field to support well-being. With over 40 years in holistic healthcare, she combines extensive training with a dedication to empowering others through understanding their bodies. Visit TheShiftDevice.com for more information.

 **Kristin Aurelia** resides in the Washington, DC metropolitan area. She is an author, host of the *Surviving the Human Experience* Podcast, Health and Wellness Coach, Reiki Master and Speaker. Her life's mission is to share experiences and bring wisdom and knowledge to the forefront of her works. www.shewisepublications.com or www.shewisewellness.com

Mariena Johnson is an 18-year-old law student at Cooley Law School, expected to graduate in 2026. She was elected to be a 1L Senator of the Student Bar Association. She received her Bachelor of Arts degree in Criminology from the University of South Florida in 2023 at the age of 17. She was a Team USA member for inline speedskating and attended the World Championships in Italy in 2023, where she skated the  marathon race. She was also a member of the Lumina Youth Choirs and got to perform at Carnegie Hall in New York City.

 **Mark Heidt** is an award-winning writer, director, producer of $30 Million in half-hour infomercials. He has a BS from Syracuse University and the State University of NY College of Environmental Science and Forestry. He has performed music at Carnegie Hall and fought forest fires in Idaho.
Mark is the husband of Sandy, the father of Ken and Ruth, and the grandfather of Graeme. He has a unique perspective on the influences that enlighten, empower, and motivate people to take effective action. His faith is above all.

Mary Vovers Brown, founder of TriMedia3, offers digital marketing to small businesses. Her corporate background has honed her communication, strategic planning, problem-solving, and creativity skills. Originally from Australia, Mary has been fortunate to live and work throughout the US including Hawaii and Alaska. She is the proud single mother of two incredible souls. Reach her at: mary@trimedia3.com

How do you describe a woman who understands the rigors of life more than most? **Michelle Harwood-Lange**'s experience stretches the gamut of exquisite joy to some serious life lessons none of us will see, even over a lifetime. She has learned to pivot those negatives into positive strengths. As an author, artist, and inspiring thought leader, her mission is to share her life through the power of the written word and visual art. Her powerful wisdom and intuition flow from a pen or brush to enlighten minds and awaken souls.

As an Army Veteran and a nurse with over 20 years of experience, **Sally Mary de Leon** approaches healing and empowerment like a master gardener, tending to each individual's needs with compassion and expertise. From patching scraped knees as a child to advocating for patients' rights as a nurse and paralegal, she has always had an innate drive to care for others. Her commitment extends to serving on non-profit boards focused on reducing veteran suicide and homelessness. Inspired by her journey, are you ready to unearth your potential for healing and growth? Visit www.operationbetterme.com to learn more.

Rev. Maj. Sandra Kitt retired US Army Major, minister, author, coach, served during Desert Storm. In 2011, Neuroleptic Malignant Syndrome left her paralyzed. She now walks, talks, drives, swims, skis, is part of the First Unity Ministry team in St. Pete, Fl. and helps people thrive. http://www.RevMajSandraKitt.com

Will Pollock is a freelance multimedia journalist, researcher, and author in Atlanta. He's a contributor to TrumpFile.org and founder of CrankyYank.com, an online news magazine. A native of New York City, now domesticated in the South, Will is a proud dad to Cameron and Jackson, a Rat Terrier puppy. He's a lifelong tennis player and fan of The New York Yankees, despite the scourge of Alex Rodriguez. Will's  fundraising effort, ARTvision Atlanta, and book Pizza for Good have raised over $100,000 for various charities.

 As a dedicated health professional, **Dr. Teresa Lynch** helps others thrive naturally, guiding clients toward their fullest potential in unique and meaningful ways. At every step of the journey, she provides support, encouragement, and tools for transformation. It's not about her but about her clients' victories. Together, they focus on nurturing the body, mind, and spirit for lasting wellness. Whether it's gaining energy, finding balance, or achieving natural health goals, her clients' success is her mission. Every win brings each client closer to a healthier, happier life." www.TeresaLynch.com

Contributing Authors

Angi Currier is a best-selling author and medical Patient Access Representative. She has three children and a granddaughter. She hopes to inspire others with her triumph over addiction. Angi feels like she has lived two lives. The first life involves physical and emotional struggles, and the second is living in gratitude, acceptance, and confidence. ajhinkle5@yahoo.com

In painting and a writing, we perceive our own reality, a glimpse of life's intangibility – the dark, the light, the movement, the continuance. From that perception, **Anne O'Brien** abstracts outcomes, without interference from the real, reflecting universality, individuality, emotion. That gives her work life and movement, evoking a world of one's own interpretation.

Dr. Anne Worth is a Christian counselor, author, workshop leader, and speaker. Anne has a heart for those who are lost or forgotten, including doggies. Her memoir, *Call me Worthy*, and her book series for children (*Tessie's Tears*) are available on Amazon. She lives in Dallas.
www.dranneworthauthor.com

Beth Fitzgerald is an executive coach, a member of the Forbes Coaches Council, a certified John Maxwell coach, blogger, master EFT practitioner, international speaker and trainer, and author of the motivational book -*The Wake Up Call.*
Beth is also a wife and mother of four children. She lives in Hoboken, NJ, and is a Rutgers University graduate.

Beth Goodman, Dr. is a Visionary, Entrepreneur, Speaker, Breast Cancer SurTHRIVER, and life Advancement Coach. Her mission is to cultivate confidence in women to accept themselves in God's image. She believes that confidence should not be a difficult goal but a fundamental aspect of everyday life.

Beth Johnston is the oldest daughter in a large family; Beth Johnston was born into management! Beth has spent her professional years reorganizing existing companies using her practical and logical perspectives to help companies achieve their highest profit years. She is known for her keen listening skills and inspiring interview techniques, now shared on **B.E.P. TALKS**. Beth can be reached at info@beptalks.com.

 BJ Largent, born and raised in Ohio, moved west for the open spaces and blue skies. With a career in media sales, she remains active in her community, serving on boards and volunteering. At 80, she still enjoys horses, did the Pony Express Re-ride, and embraces each day with gratitude and joy.

Brenda Warren the Soulutionist, is a Retired Marine with over three decades of experience in leadership, self-care, spiritual growth, and cultivating healthy relationships. Three-time best-selling author, pattern for living, and self-publishing coach. Brenda has helped countless individuals transform their lives using her innovative TAPIN Method™ (Transformation Announce Prepare Imagine Nurture). www.brendathesoulutionist.com

 Chevi Price is a motivational speaker who advocates for mental health and disabilities. She is also a new author and has always loved writing. She is using her voice, both spoken and written, without letting her physical disability define her. Chevi is conquering life one day at a time.

Christopher Crouse is a true Renaissance man. He is a business owner, minister, and writer/ author. He loves teaching and performing drama, preaching, writing, painting, drawing, singing, and playing bass guitar. Most importantly, he loves Jesus, his wife Jenn, and his children and grandchildren. Chris@ChrisCrouse.com

 Cyndi Wilkins practices the art and science of therapeutic massage and energetic bodywork for over twenty years. Her approach to healing is recognizing the mind and body work as one system. She believes in the co-creation of health, reinforcing mind, body, and spirit to explore the root causes of discomfort and disease.
She shares her stories across multiple platforms as a featured contributor to BizCatalyst 360, an award-winning global media digest and guest blogger for All Things Wellness. Cyndiwilkins12@gmail.com

Debra Costanzo founded 3 in 1 Fitness by D. L. Costanzo, LLC in July 2008, earning her health coaching certification through the Institute of Integrative Nutrition. Debra helps women over forty to incorporate mindful lifestyle changes, supporting them to live healthy, energetic lives. Debra resides in Charlotte, NC. www.3in1fitness.com

Dennis Pitocco, founder and CEO of 360° Nation, and his wife Ali, Chief Inspiration Officer, promote global positivity through ventures like BizCatalyst 360°, 360°Nation Studios, and GoodWorks 360°. Their mission prioritizes service, community benefit, and ethical media. As a bestselling contributing author, Dennis embodies responsible stewardship and showcases media potential for positive change.

Donna Franklin, an award-winning real estate agent with 17 years of experience, is also a best-selling author and celebrated entrepreneur. Driven by her own experiences of childhood hunger, she created a program that has fed 2,000 children. As an inspiring speaker, Donna advocates for addressing child hunger and overcoming adversity.

Donna Guary is a California children's author and Air Force veteran. Author of "*Broccoli! It's My Favorite Vegetable*" and "*Where in the World Does Broccoli Come From?*", she weaves history into stories encouraging children to love vegetables. A contributor to the "*Daily Gift Book Series*," she's pursuing her MA in Leadership.

Eileen Bild is CEO of Ordinary to Extraordinary Life, Founder of the Core Thinking Blueprint Method, Breakthrough S.P.A.R.K. Coach, Mentor, Author, Keynote Speaker and Internationally Syndicated Columnist. She holds a Masters in Transpersonal Psychology and is host for OTEL Talk. She helps others live their best lives and become unstoppable!

Gloria Sloan, founder and CEO of Personal Dynamics, Inc., has over four decades of experience in personal development, human resilience, and leadership service. Her expertise has empowered countless individuals to harness essential life skills for personal and professional growth. With a strong strategic business management and human resources background, Gloria delivers impactful international coaching and mentoring. As a dynamic speaker and facilitator, she inspires transformative self-discovery and growth by offering clear, practical approaches aligning core values with goals. An award-winning author, Gloria's "*Life Skills for the Journey*" is in its second edition. She hosts The Gloria Show podcast and contributes to Brainz Magazine and the *Daily Gift Book Series*.

Jacki Long is a contributing author in five books, including bestseller, *Win the Wellness W.A.R...We are Responsible for All Things Wellness.* She is a Certified Jack Canfield Success Principles Trainer, NLP practitioner, and Master Coach. Jacki customizes programs for clients, helping them achieve their highest personal and professional goals.

 Jane McCarter-Caponigro, a native New Yorker, is passionate about empowering children to embrace their uniqueness through her books. Her work fosters conversations between adults and children, encouraging curiosity, confidence, and self-worth. Jane aspires to continue uplifting young minds through her "*YES!* books" series.

Jill Clay is a Christian Leader and Coach dedicated to helping overwhelmed women heal from emotional and spiritual wounds. Using practical tools and biblical principles, she guides clients to discover their SOUL FUEL, unlocking true freedom and clarity. With 30+ years of Human Resource experience, Jill expertise in mentoring and coaching helps empower women to unlock their God-given purpose.

 Jodie Fitzgerald is a Licensed Family Dog Mediator ®, owner of Fitz Your Dog Training and a former nurse. After working with dog rescue for 5 years, she is dedicated to educating dog lovers about the dogs' truth and creating amazing relationships that will keep dogs in home living in harmony with their families.

Johnny Tan is an Experiential Keynote Speaker, Executive Career & Life Coach, Mentor, Multi-Award-Winning and Bestselling Author, Talk Show Host, Social Entrepreneur, Founder & CEO of From My Mama's Kitchen® Organization and Words Have Power store, Publisher of "Inspirations for Better Living" digital magazine, and a REIKI Master Teacher & Healer.

 Joyce Waring is a retired LPN and Special Needs Para-educator. She enjoys writing, reading, gardening, walking her Labrador, and spending time with her husband, children and grandchildren in Central Oregon's high desert. She is Chaplain for COFRW and an active member of Trinity Lutheran in Bend, OR.

Karen Booze, a former homeschool mom, is pursuing a master's degree in church ministry. She has been involved in women's ministry for nearly 20 years. A passionate student of The Word, she also enjoys reading historical fiction, camping, and spending time with her family.

Kate Rohauer lives in Sisters, Oregon. She has a master's in Christian counseling. She's the Founder of Royal Touch Grief Outreach, and a contact person for Parents of Murdered Children. A great-grandmother who loves family, friends, and her husband of 40 years. Enjoys photography, crafts and gardening.

Katerina Pappas (LadyMoon) was born in Philadelphia and raised in Greece.Her journey started at the David. A. Clarke School of Law followed by the Institute for Integrative Nutrition, and finally, receiving her teaching certificate in Kundalini yoga, from Yoga Farm Ithaca. After many years of collecting life experiences, she is infusing all her lessons into her first true loves; creative writing and singing. You can find her children's books and original songs at: ladymoonsongbooks.com

Katie Lesesne is a writer, educator, youtuber and voiceover artist based on the east coast. Over the years kindness has made a big difference in her life and it is something she works to practice every day. For more information please and to inquire about any voiceover needs visit www.katielesesne.com.

Laurie Rowland is a Poet, Author, and Coach. For 35 years, her passion has been helping women achieve transformation and breakthrough in their personal struggles so they can walk in victory. Laurie's poem, In His Image, was put to song by Casey Kearny and is available on most streaming platforms.

Linda B. Kaye owns InterActive Synergy, a Digital Marketing Agency. For 20+ years she has been helping clients sell online. She's passionate about fostering online positivity that inspires both personal and business growth. Linda is a U.S. Army Veteran and holds an MBA and Marketing Certificate from Southern NH University.

Linda Weller is the proud owner of Info Advantage, an MSP company in Rochester NY. She lives in Albion NY with her husband Mitch and poodle clan, including her favorite mini-poodle Captain Jack. Linda is the mother of three adult children and spends her free time training for Disney races.

Linette Rainville, Jesus girl, USN Veteran and Movement Leader, is on a quest to raise up the next generation of Esthers. As a podcast host, mentor and founder of Daughters United, a global equipping ministry, she empowers women to build projects and start ministries from the ground up. With 25 years of hands-on poverty outreach experience, Linette has coached thousands of Kingdom women, guiding them to pursue their callings, lead movements, and build missions.

Lori Walker is a Usui Reiki Master, Holy Fire Reiki Master and a contributing author to multiple books including *Mayhem to Miracles, The Four-Fold Formula for All Things Wellness, Wellness GPS* and *A Daily Gift of Hope*. She has worked in the commercial printing industry for over 25 years. In 2022, she was commissioned as notary public in the state of Pennsylvania.

Lucia Murphy is a dynamic creator and entrepreneur, passionate about travel, food, and adventure. As co-host of "Life with Lucia & Glynn," she shares exciting journeys with her audience. With a zest for life and a heart for new experiences, Lucia inspires others to embrace exploration and joy.

Mark Nelson O'Brien is the principal of O'Brien Communications Group https://obriencg.com/ a B2B brand-management and marketing firm he founded in 2004. He's also the co-founder and President of EinSource. And he's a lifelong writer. You can see all of his published work on Amazon.

Markus Wettstein. M.D. has practiced endocrinology for thirty years. He is a diabetes, metabolic and stress management specialist. He also works in energy medicine as a Licensed Bio-Well practitioner. He assists clients in improving their health and wellness by measuring their energy field, stress level, health status, and energy reserve via electro photonic imaging. mwettst@gmail.com

Mick Vovers, born in outback Australia, worked on Merino sheep stations and studied agriculture before exploring the world with an oil exploration company. His adventures inspired his creativity through photography, painting, writing, and storytelling. He has exhibited globally and is an internationally published author. Visit his upcoming website: mickvovers.com.

Nicola King's passion for Jesus and love for God's people drive everything she does. As a realtor, author, and leadership coach, she helps others thrive while expanding God's Kingdom. With a heart for "knowing Him and making Him known," Nicola reflects God's love through her mission work, both locally and abroad, especially in serving the homeless.

Pastor Jack Rehill has been married to his wife Patricia for 53 years, and is the father to four children and grandfather to three. Jack is the author of *The Advocate & The Adversary*, and the soon to be released book entitled *The Mediator* slated for publication in the winter of '24.

Dr. Rachelle Simpson Sweet is a certified epigenetic coach with a background in neuropsychology, specializing in personalized wellness through genetics. As an author and contributor to four books, she integrates mental, physical, and emotional health. Passionate about helping others thrive, she inspires them to embrace customized health solutions for optimal well-being. www.drrachellesweet.com

Renea Attaway is a Bible Teacher, Speaker, and Author with a background in healthcare and culinary arts. She is the CEO of Destiny by Grace Inc., a ministry dedicated to empowering individuals. With 35 years in ministry and 24 in business leadership, she helps others overcome challenges through faith and practical skills.

Renée Isermann is the founder and international bestselling author of Yoga4Face®. Ten thousand international clients have learned ways to rebalance their faces to reveal more beauty naturally. She believes beauty comes from within and has spent 30 years honing her skill and knowledge to become the leading expert on naturally and holistically revealing that beauty. Learn more at www.yoga4face.com

Rhonda Douglas Charles is the immigrant career strategist and founder of Adnohr Docs in Brooklyn, NY, who champions professional growth for 1st and 2nd-generation immigrants. With 25+ years of providing career services, she has guided everyone from new grads to top execs. An immigrant herself, Rhonda's mission is to ease the transformation from survival jobs to thriving careers.

Rutez Mason LeViege, Native of New Orleans, LA., has been a nurse for over 24 years. She now serves as Director of Health & Wellness. An ordained minister and mentor, Rutez is Brad LeViege's wife, Frederick, Destin, and Elijah's mother and the grandmother of Markenzi. Rutez will release her first children's book by December 2024.

Shaheda Daya helps individuals overcome anxiety to discover their true potential with positivity and compassion. With over 25 years in the corporate world and personal experience overcoming anxiety and depression, I guide clients to trust themselves, uncover their inner wisdom, and build resilience for personal and professional growth.

Sophia Long is a scholar studying sociology and women, gender, and sexuality studies at IUPUI. She is an avid activist and intersectional feminist, currently living in the Midwest with her partner and two cats. sophialongwrites@gmail.com

Terry Scarborough, 67, lives on Maryland's eastern shore. Widowed after 31 years of marriage to Gary, a Baptist pastor, she has two daughters, Lauren and Hannah. Terry adores her three grandchildren: Grady, Mae, and Sunny. She loves being a Gigi and serving in ministry whenever possible.

Tyra Glaze is a 11-year Triple Negative Breast Cancer Warrior. She's the Author of a children's book "My Mom is My Hero." Tyra is the proud mother of two young men: Tae (19) and Que (16). She's been featured on Susan Komen and Torrid sharing her journey through breast cancer.

Meet the Author
Teresa Velardi

Teresa is a bestselling author, publisher, host of the *Conversations That Make a Difference* podcast, coach, and potter.

Michaelangelo, the famous 15th-century artist and sculptor said, *Every block of stone has a statue inside it, and it is the sculptor's task to discover it.* His job was to remove the excess stone to reveal the beauty within.

Similarly, Teresa uses the art of pottery to illustrate that each ball of clay can and will be transformed into a beautiful work of art with the touch of the potter's hand. Teresa guides her clients through the process of centering, molding, shaping, and walking through the fire of challenges to effect positive life change as they gracefully and powerfully embrace the work of art they already are.

Teresa found her passion and purpose through life's challenges while trusting God's plan. Faith in God, gratitude, and giving are her heart. Her abilities as a writer, editor, and publisher are vital ingredients she brings to those who share their message with the world on her podcast or through her publishing platform.

Her daily quiet time, writing, and gratitude practice keep Teresa focused on her God-given purpose as life unfolds in this ever-changing world. We all have a story to tell and a heartfelt message to share. What's your message?

https://linktr.ee/teresavelardi.

Meet the Foreword
P.J.

P.J. is an International Speaker and Resiliency Expert! He has delivered more than 4,000 presentations in his lifetime and is considered one of the world's leading authorities on overcoming obstacles. At 19, he was the youngest person to be inducted into the National Hall of Fame for People with Disabilities and has been seen by—and/or worked with—people in more than 35 countries.

Despite P.J.'s disability, he has lived an extraordinary life: painting, sailing, training in martial arts, outdoor skydiving, indoor skydiving, trapezing, ziplining, hiking, mountain climbing, snow skiing, water skiing, aqua jetpacking, playing wheelchair sports, and the list goes on! https://www.pjswisdom.com/

Meet the Afterword
Martariesa Logue

Martariesa Logue, born with TAR syndrome, overcame early medical challenges with faith and resilience. She is Assistant Director of the Virtual Learning Academy, cofounder of the Ohio Valley Youth Network, and involved with the Sycamore Youth and Community Center. Passionate about technology and service, she leads her church's Tech Team. Raised with a sense of independence, Martariesa sees challenges as opportunities for growth. Guided by the mantra "Thy will be done," she lives with purpose and dedication. Married to John, with a daughter, two beagles, and a hedgehog, Martariesa enjoys family time and continues to inspire others.

Kindness Story Take-Aways

Name of Story:

Author:

How I connected to the Story:

Kindness Story Take-Aways

Name of Story:

Author:

How I connected to the Story:

Kindness Story Take-Aways

Name of Story:

Author:

How I connected to the Story:

Kindness Story Take-Aways

Name of Story:

Author:

How I connected to the Story:

Kindness Story Take-Aways

Name of Story:

Author:

How I connected to the Story:

Kindness Story Take-Aways

Name of Story:

Author:

How I connected to the Story:

Kindness Story Take-Aways

Name of Story:

Author:

How I connected to the Story:

Kindness Story Take-Aways

Name of Story:

Author:

How I connected to the Story:

Kindness Story Take-Aways

Name of Story:

Author:

How I connected to the Story:

Kindness Story Take-Aways

Name of Story:

Author:

How I connected to the Story:

Made in United States
Troutdale, OR
11/21/2024

25159437R00124